Unfurl

Survivals, Sorrows, and Dreaming

Duke University Press
Durham & London   2025

Eli Clare

Printed in the United States of America on acid-free paper ∞
Project Editor: Liz Smith
Designed by Courtney Leigh Richardson
Typeset in Garamond Premier Pro
by Copperline Book Services

Library of Congress Cataloging-in-Publication Data
Names: Clare, Eli, author.
Title: Unfurl : survivals, sorrows, and dreaming / Eli Clare.
Description: Durham : Duke University Press, 2025. | Includes
bibliographical references and index.
Identifiers: LCCN 2024057288 (print)
LCCN 2024057289 (ebook)
ISBN 9781478032410 (paperback)
ISBN 9781478029045 (hardcover)
ISBN 9781478061267 (ebook)
Subjects: LCGFT: Poetry. | Prose poems.
Classification: LCC PS3603.L352 U548 2025 (print) |
LCC PS3603.L352 (ebook) | DDC 811/.6—dc23/eng/20250528
LC record available at https://lccn.loc.gov/2024057288
LC ebook record available at https://lccn.loc.gov/2024057289

Cover art: Emerging. © Jacks McNamara, www.jacksmcnamara.net.
Cover description: A portion of Jacks McNamara's circular piece
Emerging, originally painted on a round of basswood, fills the book
cover of *Unfurl* from edge to edge. Vibrant bands of color curve
inward, forming a partial circle, the outer edges starting in the upper
and lower right corners, first with layers of maroon, red, and yellow.
Then shades of blue, infused with sunlight, bend across the cover, a
meandering river. In the lower left corner, nestled inside the blue curve,
sits a heart of roots and tendrils in green, tan, light gray, and rust red.
The book's title, *Unfurl*, printed in a large white font, floats on top of
the bands of color, intertwined with fans of what might be seeds or
stones, teardrop shaped and delicate. Underneath the book title hangs
the subtitle, *Survivals, Sorrows, and Dreaming*, and beneath those
words, the author's name, Eli Clare.

To the white pines and stones who steady me.

Contents

Acknowledgments

In these catastrophic and genocidal times, I am filled with gratitude for all the beings—nonsentient and sentient, more-than-human and human, dead and living—who make my words possible.

First and always, the land and waters, sky and stars. I wrote big chunks of this book while living outside at Ricker Pond and Mt. Philo in unceded ancestral Abenaki territory and while preoccupied by the ocean, tides, horseshoe crabs, and wind at Cherry Grove in Secatogue homeland. As a white settler and uninvited guest living on stolen Indigenous land, let me be clear: LandBack now!

In serious and ongoing collaboration, I cocreated *Unfurl* with the following rock stars: Joe Kadi, who for more than thirty years has nudged, encouraged, and supported me and my words in every way imaginable. Susan Burch, who with generosity and brilliance has read and reread many, many drafts, coauthored the index, helped me reach deep into a tangle of ideas and histories, and believed unwaveringly in my voice. Alice Sheppard and Kinetic Light, whose invitation to write for their dance performance DESCENT sparked this book and whose disability art, kindness, and rigor reverberate on every page. And Samuel Lurie, who wakes up with me every morning, holds me through the easy bits and the tough bits, and loves me so well. Gratitudes beyond gratitude.

As I wrote, death swirled close; almost two dozen people in my life—some of them close, others farther away, and all of them influential in one way or another—died. I miss many of them beyond words. Their presence is folded into these pages. I call their names. I send unending gratitude into the cosmos particularly to Amber Hollibaugh, Carrie Ann Lucas, Laura Hershey, Laura Rauscher, PJ Redbird Two Ravens, and Stacey Park Milbern.

And the living, oh, the living. Gratitude to the elders in my life: Suzanne Pharr, who has known me since I was six months old; Corbett O'Toole; and Aurora Levins Morales.

Gratitude to the people who read drafts and whose feedback strengthened my ideas and stories and how I thought about access: Susan Raffo, Curtis Walker, Cal Montgomery, Alison Kafer, Julia Watts Belser, Rebecca Denison, Kevin Gotkin, Georgina Kleege, Catherine Kudlick, Ian Sutherland, and all the folks at Duke University Press, particularly Elizabeth Ault.

Gratitude to the people whose lives, work, and friendship make my life more possible: Adrianne Neff, Akemi Nishida, Alison Kafer, Annette Marcus, Carla Grayson, Deirdre Kelly, Ellen Samuels, Gabriel Arkles, Heba Nimr, Lezlie Frye, Loree Erickson, Lynne Whitney, Margaret Price, Mel Chen, Merri Rose, Patricia Fontaine, Rebecca Widom, Sarah Paige, Sebastian Margaret, Sunaura Taylor, Susan Raffo, Susan Stinson, Syrus Marcus Ware, Tammie Johnson, and Tracy Bartlett.

And finally, gratitude to the BIPOC (Black, Indigenous, and other people of color) Disability Justice activists and cultural workers whose art, organizing, and thinking make so much survival and dreaming possible, both in my world and on my bookshelves. Among many others, let me name Alice Wong, Anita Cameron, Emi Koyama, JJJJJerome Ellis, Jen Deerinwater, Jina Kim, Lateef McLeod, Leah Lakshmi Piepzna-Samarasinha, Ly Xīnzhèn Zhǎngsūn, Patricia Berne, Sami Schalk, Sandie (Chun Shan) Yi, Sandy Ho, and Talila A. Lewis.

. . . . .

In different forms, earlier versions of some of the pieces in this volume appeared in a variety of anthologies, journals, periodicals, and websites:

"Kisses, Fists, and Underground Rivers" and "Lake Champlain at Flood Level" in *Troubling the Line: Trans and Genderqueer Poetry and Poetics*, edited by TC Tolbert and Trace Peterson (Nightboat, 2013)

"Dailiness" and "Sugar Maple" in *Strange Mutualisms*, edited by Corinne Teed (Vernal Pond Press, 2024)

"Moving Close to the Ground: A Messy Love Song" in *Moving Mountains: Writing Nature Through Illness and Disability*, edited by Louise Kenward (Footnote, 2023)

"The Art of Disassociation" in *Split This Rock*'s Poem of the Week series, https://www.splitthisrock.org/poetry-database/poem/the-art-of -disassociation

"Creating Categories" in *Narrative Art and the Politics of Health*, edited by Neil Brooks and Sarah Blanchette (Anthem, 2021)

"A Great Flock of Stories (1977, 504 Sit-In)" in the exhibit *Patient No More: People with Disabilities Securing Civil Rights*, https://longmoreinstitute.sfsu.edu/patient-no-more/we-need-great-flock-stories

"May Day (2020)" in the *South Atlantic Quarterly* 120, no. 2 (2021): 255–56

"Bear" in the *Writer's Chronicle* 53, no. 4 (2021): 43

A Cluster of Practices AN INTRODUCTION

Practice: A routine. A repetition. A learning. A commitment. A deepening. A cluster of practices shapes *Unfurl: Survivals, Sorrows, and Dreaming.*

. . . . .

a practice of remembering:

Time loops and swirls through these pages. Memory unfurls into the past-present-future, a phrase I use with great intention. In this practice of remembering, time does not travel in straight lines. Instead it swings wide. Arcs, twists, folds into itself. Wails long notes and short, an accordion gathering and releasing their breath.

I remember tremors as old as dolomite scraping over shale. Remember history as sweeping as the US Homestead Act of 1862. As personal as the federal government giving my great-granduncle 160 acres of stolen Sisseton-Wahpeton Dakota land. I remember white pine and sugar maple as kin. Remember rebellion and love.

This practice expands to the Milky Way. Contracts to my tremoring hands smeared with muck. Functions on many different scales and scopes. Idiosyncratic and incomplete. Full of absence as well as presence.

. . . . .

a practice of survival and sorrow:

Survival and sorrow crouch in every corner of *Unfurl*. These pieces emerged during a time of ongoing upheaval. Bees and bears live on the edge of extinction. Refugees trudge through the snow. Many of us navigate the everyday aftermaths of violence and death.

As I wrote, my words looped me back into old survivals and sorrows, past-present-future pouring into each other. I returned to the early years of the AIDS epidemic (1981–83) as I was coming out. Until effective life-saving drugs became available fifteen years later, that disease killed people of all genders by the thousands—particularly, in my world, gay and bi men. I remember my young queer self surrounded by unrelenting funerals.

In that decade and a half, death cascading around us, we sat in community and called the names of people lost to AIDS. Wave after wave—ten minutes, a half hour, sometimes an hour before we'd fall silent—the space flooding with an ocean of names.

AIDS to COVID-19, epidemic to epidemic, war to war, hurricane to fire: The dead keep piling up. Living with a broken heart has become familiar and common, a long-haul reality, not a temporary condition. This book is a calling of the names, a practice of survival and sorrow.

. . . . .

a practice of porousness:

My broken heart, skin, words practice porousness. Boundaries between human and more-than-human dissolve. Granite and aspen, pelican and beaver become kin. Sentient and nonsentient merge.

This practice blurs prose and poetry. Blends emotion, analysis, story. Uses citations to interlace different kinds of knowledge—kitchen table conversations, academically published histories, gratitudes to white pine and full moon.

Categories collapse and fail. Portals open into unclassifiable futures. I unfurl myself and invite you to join me in this endeavor, by turns demanding and joyful, unexpected and risky.

. . . . .

a practice of dreaming:

I dream and dream and dream in these pages, tapping into multiple modes of imagining—tasting, smelling, tactile sensing, intuiting, listening, moving. I practice dreaming as survival, pleasure, and rebellion. Claim as essential both the quirky ephemeral currents of sleep time and the rebellious utopian desires of waking time.

Many of us practice dreaming in the quiet of our slumber. But this work, particularly daytime justice dreaming, is also collective and communal. A skill we teach each other. A practice we cultivate together.

. . . . .

Writing this book over the last seven years has nourished me. Invited me to live more fully in my broken heart. Encouraged me to slip more often into rocks and trees. Enticed me to dream ferocious and tender rebellions.

May these words also nourish you.

June 2024
Basin of Lake Champlain, unceded ancestral Abenaki territory

Access Practices

Access practices ground *Unfurl*. When I tell you about access, I'm turning toward the logistics of reading/listening to/absorbing this book. But even more crucially, I'm telling you about the bedrock. The communal practices of accessible language, multiple formats, content notes, pauses, and more shape every page. They influence my words. They inform my ideas. They structure my stanzas and paragraphs. And they may determine how (or if) you read this book.

These practices are collective processes (not items on a checklist), guided by general principles, and manifested in hundreds of details. We learn them from each other.

Accessible Language

Decades ago I committed myself to accessible language—words that hold the front door wide open. I started learning this practice not in cross-disability spaces but from community-based feminist writers, many of them lesbians of color, in the 1980s and early '90s. Through their work, they showed me the possibilities of mixing genres with wild abandon and using unadorned language in nuanced ways. Over time I came to know that accessible language also works in tandem with the disability access practices of live/open/closed captions, written and spoken materials made available in multiple formats, and signed language interpretation.

My commitment to using unadorned language in nuanced ways has led me to story-based critical analysis, a reliance on metaphor, and an insistence on sensory bodymind-based experience. I intentionally avoid academic jargon. Those words, arising from specialized areas of study, often have convoluted meanings and function to shut many people out. I can never remember their definitions. Trying to read them feels like running into a brick wall.

The poetry in *Unfurl* may feel, to some readers, the same way—a headlong crash into some unyielding barrier. If that reality is true for you, try reading or listening to the poems as if they were unfamiliar foods or dance moves that leave you confused, skeptical, and curious all at the same time. Give yourself space; experiment: They might spark (or not). Maybe you'll catch the feelings and miss the meanings or wrestle with both. However you absorb this book, you are neither wrong nor "stupid"—that word itself, a tool of ableist-sexist-antipoor white supremacy. The poems here are not puzzles with one correct solution and many incorrect ones. Instead they are practices of dreaming and porousness—idiosyncratic, full of kinships, structured not by logic but by rhythm, sound, sensation, emotion.

Gratitudes, Citations, and Other Notes

I want to fling the front door of *Unfurl* wide open. To this end, I've written several kinds of notes.

FORMAT NOTES: Some of my poems (and occasionally my prose) swirl across the page in ways readers may not expect or find visually accessible. Lines cascade, rupture, hug the right margin rather than the left. I've included "format notes" underneath the titles of these pieces. Think of them as maps or verbal descriptions of the shapes the poems make. I wrote these notes into the main body of *Unfurl* (rather than as alt text, which is available only to people using screen readers) in order to create more access for a variety of readers. They are experiments in an access practice I've not encountered before. As such, I know they're messy, rudimentary, and incomplete. Of course I hope they'll be useful to readers. But I also hope they will encourage other writers to adopt and further develop this access practice.

HISTORICAL NOTES: Sometimes I reference events or histories that I don't explain in the text and that readers may be unfamiliar with. In these cases, I include "historical notes" (located again underneath individual titles) to provide some context for my stories and images.

DEFINITIONS: In many ways, the practice of accessible language revolves around definitions. Which ones open the door, and which slam it tight? These questions become tricky in this genre-bending book. I choose not to define *ableism, settler colonialism, white supremacy, capitalism, patriarchy, transphobia*, *homophobia*, and more in the main body of the text. I want them to be understood and felt not through sharp, crisp definition but in story, experience, and accumulated community wisdom. Yet I know definitions create more access for some readers. To this end, I place a handful of definitions in the unnumbered endnotes at the back of the book.

CITATIONS: Academic writers and scholars come from traditions that expect notes at the bottoms of pages and ends of books (otherwise known as citations) to map out scholarly sources, origins, influences, and tangents to their arguments/ideas/histories/analyses/theories/data. These notes are often used to build academic credibility and authority. I, on the other hand, come from writing traditions that don't consider citations, beyond crediting direct quotes, important at all.

But in this book, I use endnotes widely. I braid together the largely land-, community-, and activist-based webs of relationships (both human and more-than-human) that pull my words into existence. I define; I thank; I cite art, conversations, ecosystems, rocks, trees, books, zines, websites, films, social media threads, articles, and more. I'm not joining an academic tradition but instead claiming citations as a community-based practice of interdependence, gratitude, and access.

CONTENT NOTES (AKA CONTENT OR TRIGGER WARNINGS): See below for details.

Access Practices Are Never Complete

Access practices—these communal skills we're teaching each other—are almost always incomplete and flawed. For example, as deeply as I've committed to and practiced accessible language, I don't, in these pages, embrace the specific standards of plain language. Defined by guidelines about word choice, sentence and paragraph structure, and document design, plain language creates communication access for many different groups of people. Originally developed in a variety of contexts, including manufacturing and government work, these standards have, more recently, been adopted and further developed as disability access by intellectually/developmentally disabled people, autistic people, self-advocates, and allies.

Simply put, plain language is structured, specific, and rigorous in ways that my current practice of accessible language is not. It holds the front door open even further. I want to begin leaning in to this rigor. What poems, ideas, relationships, and activist strategies might I find through using plain language standards to shape my words?

For now, I imagine *Unfurl* as a hard-copy book printed in a sans-serif font alongside a plain language edition; an audiobook; a braille version; a screen-readable e-book; a free-of-charge, fully searchable PDF; and an ASL (American Sign Language) video. Some of these editions exist, but others do not. Not yet, that is. I dream of a not-so-distant past-present-future when all of these formats are published simultaneously as a matter of course.

Not Complete but Still Necessary

Sometimes I watch people use the frequent incompleteness of access practices as an excuse not to engage in access work at all. But our routines don't need to be complete or perfect to be useful. Instead we need to keep creating, hacking, problem solving, and being accountable as we center access.

Every time I use or create content notes, I think about prioritizing usefulness. The practice of content notes, naming potential triggers, not as a way of trying to control impact but as an act of collective care, will always be vexingly incomplete. We can never comprehensively predict and name everyone's triggers.

But at the same time, this practice is so useful. I started learning about it decades ago as an activist in the feminist antiviolence movement. Trigger warnings (also known now as content notes or content warnings) gave me as a survivor just enough access to stay present and engaged when our work turned to graphic details of sexual assault and domestic violence. Today I regularly both create and use content notes in a variety of contexts, working in the spirit of useful and incomplete.

Content Notes and Care

Writing content notes for *Unfurl* has been particularly confounding. These pages place daily interpersonal ableism next to flashbacks of childhood abuse, rebellion next to joy, community connection next to climate chaos. Accounts and analysis of ableism, racism, sexism, homophobia, transphobia, capitalism, settler colonialism, and environmental destruction appear throughout the book. In other words, I could tag almost every piece here with a content note.

None of what I've written contains extended descriptions of—or gratuitous details about—trauma, violence, or death. But I do directly and vividly name these experiences alongside survival, community, kinship, joy, beauty, resistance, rebellion, dreaming of liberation, and releasing of past trauma.

After hours of thinking and conversation with other writers and activists, I still have not successfully answered the question of what to tag and how. My desire is, of course, to provide useful prompts toward self- and collective care. But tagging every piece simply wouldn't help us know how and when to take care of ourselves and each other.

In writing this book, I leaned hard into self-care. The themes of trauma, violence, and death rumbled in my bones 24/7. Time often wavered and cracked. I paused again and again, making space to walk, drink water, cook, curl into a tree, breathe, nap.

And so, I weave my practice of pauses into these pages. Specifically, I punctuate section II, which is focused on grief and trauma, with short poem-reminders that begin with "pause   pause." Consider them poetic access breaks. Please put the book down, dog-ear or bookmark pages to return to, skip what feels like too much. In other words, I'm encouraging you to develop your own practice of pauses.

In the end, I decided not to tag individual pieces. Instead, I include general content notes at the bottom of each section's title page (pages 1, 17, 33, 61, 81, and 105). In these notes, I pay particular attention to the naming of significant trauma, violence, and death. I hope they are useful both as flags and as prompts toward self- and collective care.

. . . . .

Practice: A routine. A repetition. A learning. A commitment. A deepening.

I dream of a world where practices of access, interdependence, and collective care are so common, so at the center of everything, so woven into every day that we frequently have no need to even name them. In the meantime, let's keep practicing.

Prelude

Kisses, Fists, and Underground Rivers

HISTORICAL NOTE: *The fourth part of this poem centers on the 1986 Great Peace March. Over the course of eight and a half months, I walked, along with hundreds of other people, across the United States for global nuclear disarmament. In the 1980s, the Cold War seemed endless. The federal government exploded a nuclear weapon at the Nevada Test Site once every three weeks. Missile silos, staffed twenty-four hours a day, ready to launch nuclear warheads aimed at the Soviet Union, dotted the Great Plains. We talked peace, taught peace, tried to live peace with each other in our mobile tent city. Not simply an absence of war in a world long steeped in armed conflict, massacre, and genocide, peace with justice was, and still is, both a radical imagining of the future and a daily practice in the present.*

Because poems live in cracks, crevices, fissures.

Take root after landslides and wildfires—pale green of huckleberry already unfurling.

Because they churn upstream to their spawning beds.

Dapple the ground with sunlight.

Roll in the surf, grip the rocks, hunker over coffee at 4 a.m. before another fourteen-hour day.

. . . . .

1979: I sat in sixth-period study hall, bored out of my mind. The only alternative—Mr. Beckman's poetry class—held no appeal. But restless and desperate, I decided to take a chance.

We scribbled poems in spiral-bound notebooks. Sent them out for publication. Collected rejection letters.

Read William Carlos Williams and Emily Dickinson but not June Jordan or Lucille Clifton.

In that tiny backwoods high school, no one studied AP English or received a National Merit Scholarship. We ended up single mothers and grocery store clerks, gas station attendants and regulars at Pitch's Tavern.

We organized fieldtrips. Drove hundreds of miles. Heard Carolyn Kizer, Galway Kinnell, Gary Snyder read their poems. Saved our pocket change to buy their books.

Poetry grabbed me by the collar, whispered in my ear, "You're comin' with me." I followed willingly, destination unknown.

. . . . .

Because poems are kisses, fists, and underground rivers.

. . . . .

1986: Twenty-two years old and unsure whether my poet-activist voice would ever be of use, I joined the Great Peace March: Los Angeles to Washington, DC, 3,700 miles for global nuclear disarmament.

I dreamed, walked, woke up with poems. Wrote about the Nevada Test Site and the Seneca Army Depot, meltdowns at Chernobyl and Three Mile Island. Words clamoring and insistent.

We read poems at peace rallies. Sang songs in church basements. Told stories in greasy spoon cafés.

Mojave blooming yellow in April, cornfields growing lush and tasseled in August: I memorized my poems. Stepped up to the microphone. Didn't feel bold.

At those rallies and coffeehouses, my voice stumbled and cracked, sometimes beginning to carry.

. . . . .

Because poems stitch and restitch themselves across the decades. Refuse Wall Street.

Stand in line at the welfare office. Gossip, laugh, pass the word, "Don't let 'em get you down."

Because they drool, dream, panic, stim. Link arms with riotous graffiti and old protest songs.

Groan and thud, float in the dark, late at night in detention centers and psych wards.

Shout into the cosmos and keep us alive as surely as warm oatmeal in the morning.

Heart

heart of lake at flood level, heart of stone, heart of pine, heart
of glacier collapsing, heart of spasm and stim, heart of river
no longer reaching estuary, heart of scientist working
to create a vaccine for which the whole world awaits,
heart of hummingbird–hive–hay barn, heart of octopus
and damselfly, heart of ER nurse after a sixteen-hour shift,
heart of thunderhead, heart of apple tree, heart of janitor
cleaning rooms of the newly dead, heart of queerness,
heart of kindness, heart of gender rebellion, heart of falcon
nesting atop skyscraper, heart of raven, heart of tightrope
walker at 2 a.m., heart of dance floor–disco ball–drag queen
after one too many whiskey sours, heart of no justice
no peace, heart of snake–mouse–owl, heart of bedrock,
heart of treehouse, heart of grief, heart of jet stream,
heart of Milky Way, heart of sandhill crane, heart of rumble,
heart of rage, heart of hallucination, heart of hardness, heart
of slowness, heart of worry, heart of orgasm, heart of gasping
for breath, heart of ventilator, heart twitching, heart stumbling,
heart beginning to stop, beginning to break, beginning to rise.

Unfurl: An Invitation

FORMAT NOTE: *Short questions anchored to the right margin amplify the poem's invitation.*

become
stars
shadows
flickers
of light

a prowling
and tender
melody

fingertips
gripping the edge

call it home
call it desire
call it a need
to never
let go

what do we wail into the world?

. . . . .

unfurl your heart
your belly
your vertebrae
one by one

slide
into your skin

a spider
poised

. . . . .

between crests
enter the trough

fill yourself
with sunlight
and smoke

. . . . .

unfurl
your featherless
wings

brush the skin
of belly
and sternum

. . . . .

but no:

draw knees
to chest

rest bone
upon bone

how do we unlearn desperation?

. . . . .

become
a single
piercing
bell

raindrops
plucked
from a cello

stars
shadows
flickers
of light

. . . . .

learn
to slide
crouch
crawl

flat
of hand
curve of
kneecap

bone
uncushioned

. . . . .

grasp
wrench
pull

become predator
become prey

become both
or neither
a shiver of pain

do not
let go
of tenderness

. . . . .

oh, yes:
the muscle
softened   breath
deepened   throat
opened

but do not
ignore

the unfurling
itself

that arch   arc
momentum
of a full turn

. . . . .

poise
on the edge

body
leaning in

push
and descend
push
and descend

a raptor riding
the thermals

neither hunting
nor hunted

. . . . .

the moment
after gravity
takes hold

that rupture
revelation
release

what does the unfurling demand of us?

lunge

and lunge again

. . . . .

unfurl
your fingertips
your knuckles
your wrists

bend
and caress
bend
and caress

then
flick away

. . . . .

lean
into a cradle
made of wheelchair
and flesh

star
stone
feather
suspended

. . . . .

accept her invitation—
straddle her lap
become the gliding
of her wheels

the hands
twined through
her hair

. . . . .

slide into
the underworld

do not
leave

limbs writhe
bodies tangle
shadows multiply

. . . . .

wander through
a forest
of bull kelp

brush against
tongue
and tooth

whisper
whisper

history splinters

. . . . .

but no:

draw knees
to chest

rest bone
upon bone

who do we touch and how?

.....

become
a fault line
fissure
fulcrum

balance on
the earth

pause
pause

star
stone
feather
unfurling

.....

you plummet
body careening

earth
no longer
steady

pretend
it does not
matter

.....

hit ground

crack
bruise
brace

gravity
swells

. . . . .

unfurl disgust
despair
the shame
that will not
leave

descend
and collapse
descend
and collapse

. . . . .

become
a vortex

do not
relent

. . . . .

which stories do we hide away?

an aching joint
a gasping muscle

pause
pause

become tremor
become tension

become both
or neither
a shiver of light

and which stories do we brandish?

. . . . .

unfurl yourself
into wheel
and axle

body barely
touching earth

nerves registering
pressure
pain
danger

collide
and descend
collide
and descend

. . . . .

back arched
arms splayed

history
prowls
and flickers

. . . . .

bone becomes
metal becomes
skin becomes
spoke becomes
slope becomes
splinters become
stories become
sternum becomes
moan becomes
fingertip becomes
ache becomes you

do not
let go

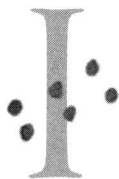

I

Tremors

CONTENT NOTES: This section interweaves rebellion, love for the more-than-human world, and connection with daily interpersonal ableism.

Your Tremoring Hands and Mine

Strangers on the street
taunt, stare, turn away:

let us forget our manners,
compliance, veneer
of politeness,

teach each other
to keen and rage,
strut and flirt,

make them yearn,
turn to look again,

make them flee,

make them remember their own shivering skin, tremulous laugh.

Remember

1.
flicker   startle
flash of motion
grip unsteady

a dailiness of tremors

2.
always
another rude
question   pitying
glance

stranger   doctor   teacher   judge   social worker   boss

in those endless
moments   our hands
remember

3.
tectonic plates hungering
for friction   heat
that long jolting rub
of rock against rock

and yet hold still   still
'til they can no longer
bear the stillness:

our hands remember
dolomite scraping
over shale

careen and shake   planets
trembling on their axes

Dailiness

a bedrock of tremors
an excitement of tremors
a river of tremors
a feather bed of tremors
a flock of tremors
a skittering at low tide
a drumming of woodpeckers
a low buzz of honeybees

subway tunnel, jackhammer, aftershock:
songs filling every chamber

Never Still: Eclipse over Ricker Pond

Moon climbs
the ladder of sky,
chill and bright,
color of butter.

She floats wavering
on the rocky bottom, catches
ripples, throws shadows

until shadow eats
her roundness, first
lopsided, then waning,

waning. Earth, moon,
sun slow dance,
a love note thrown
into the solar system.

Butter turns,
sky darkens,
moon awaits,
a burnt kernel:

pond never still.

One Long Note

a deep-throated song
shimmers

vocal cords vibrate
one long note

contract
and release,

contract
and release,

like wind
like hail

your hands and mine
wail through the world

River

water pressed
behind a dam

concrete
quivers   quivers

river of tremble
river of stumble
river of stutter
river of rage
river of quake
river of yes
river of no
river of ache
river of joy

Feather Bed

nestle
into a feather bed
of tremors

fall asleep, bodies
purring in the sun

Tremulous

might your hands
and mine

be as beautiful
as a pond
at midnight: no
wind, no
rain, current
tucked away,
asleep, yet

the surface
murmurs,

holding the moon
and her tremulous trail?

Moving Close to the Ground: A Messy Love Song

Crossing Beaver Brook, unceded ancestral Abenaki territory, late summer. The water flows, eddies, gurgles amid a tumble of boulders. I morph into a quadruped, some combination of hands, feet, and butt always touching the moss-covered rocks. Surface of the water wrinkles, smooths, wrinkles again. I linger, body cooling; the ripeness of decaying leaves, dirt, and fungi surrounds me. When I start moving again, my body lifts, reaches, inches sideways, the boulders smearing my hands with muck.

. . . . .

In disability community, we rarely talk about sliding, scooting, crawling, crab walking. We appreciate the speed of power chair users on smooth firm ground, admire the broad shoulders of manual chair users. We trade mobility techniques, talk mechanics, support each other through the bureaucracy of acquiring new gear. We relish gimpy ways of walking: the rhythm and sounds of forearm crutch users, the pure loveliness of how we decorate our canes and accessorize with them. In contrast, we seem loath to talk about, much less admire, modes of mobility that bring us close to the ground.

When we've been forced to drag ourselves up or down a flight of stairs—either in public because of outlandish inaccessibility or in private because we simply want to be with friends—we will tell stories about feeling humiliated, embarrassed, or enraged. But we don't exchange tips about sliding, when and where we scoot, how we protect our hands and wrists while crab walking. We've not shared and accumulated decades of community know-how about crawling. Those of us who move close to the ground for pleasure or utility do so mostly in isolation.

As an unsteady walkie who has a lifelong history of using these modes of mobility, I feel alone and lonely amid this disability community absence. My aloneness began early: At age two, well after my nondisabled peers had begun exploring the world on their own two feet, I gimped around on my knees, discovering treasures tucked under beds. I didn't have playmates. At age six, when my family and I lived for a summer in a basement apartment with my maternal grandparents, I perfected a scoot-slide, bumping myself down into the living room on my butt. Frustrated and half angry, my parents insisted repeatedly that I stand up and walk, even though I was petrified of falling on the stairs.

Now decades later when I face a craggy trail, a lip of rock, or a narrow bridge without handrails—my balance always a bit precarious—I often drop down onto my hands and knees. Neither a protest against ableism nor a performance of disability, moving close to the ground offers me many possibilities and connections. Muscles loosen. Pace slows. Eyes, ears, nose focus. Yet I am still alone.

I want to share these experiences with folks who will understand them both viscerally and politically. I ache for a disability love song to scooting and crawling.

·····

Kettle Pond, unceded ancestral Abenaki territory, mid-autumn. Walking over roots and rocks, slick from the morning's rain, I slow down. I concentrate. I brace myself through a stumble. My sweetie, long familiar with my pace and rhythm, offers me a hand. He knows that on this terrain I need a third point of contact to steady myself. Before accepting, I hesitate, feel a moment of conflict. A slew of ableist lies reverberate through me—*burden, clumsy, ugly*. Then, as our palms slide together, his solid stance bolstering mine, I remember: not *burden* but *love*, not *ugly* but *the quivering of aspen leaves*, not *clumsy* but *slow* and *intimate*. Our creation of access makes the roots and rocks less treacherous but still difficult—terrain that I simply need to cross.

But when I stop walking, lower my center of gravity, and scoot, these roots are no longer a barrier. Rather, they form tributaries, crevices, miniature caves cushioned in moss, calling out to me. An orange-brown newt catches my motion, holds stock-still.

·····

I have developed many ways of gaining access in the world. Certainly moving close to the ground excels as one of these strategies. But just as importantly, it leads me deeper into intimacy with the more-than-human world. Access and intimacy don't always work in tandem; the wheelchair ramp into the post office or double time on timed tests isn't necessarily created through close and abiding relationships. Likewise, access doesn't guarantee familiarity and affection. But when the two come together—access creating intimacy and in turn intimacy fostering deeper and broader access—I feel tremendous ease and belonging. The pair strengthens my closest relationships, both with humans and with trees and rocks, chipmunks and maple leaves, trillium and lichen.

·····

Lake Champlain, unceded ancestral Abenaki territory, Winter Solstice. Sculpted ice lines the shore. It coats the Monkton quartzite slabs that extend into the water and envelops the scruffy eastern red cedars growing out of the crevices. I walk, and then, after losing my balance, scoot into this winter magic. Soon my lower back and hands ache with cold that grows more intense by the minute. I slide among the cedars, absorbed in the fantastical frosted shapes, inching my way beneath the tree branches. I end up lying on my back, cradled by the frozen stone, chilled to the bone.

· · · · ·

Moving low to the ground—through mud or snow, across puddles, over gravel—can be a messy affair. In the best of conditions, my hands get scratched; my wrists, elbows, and shoulders grow sore from bearing my body weight; sharp rocks stab my hamstrings. Even so, I adore scooting. It slows me down, distance no longer measured in miles but rather in yards. I creep, inch, linger. This pace creates intimacy and space for the tiniest details: mushrooms pushing up through pine needles, spores dotting the underside of ferns, miniature icicles hanging on the tips of cedar branches.

Even with all this lovely slowness, the mud, muck, and cold undeniably create a certain kind of mess. But I want to reframe this messiness because the persistent difficulty for me actually has little to do with the physicality of scooting. Ableism, and the ways it privileges strong, steady, unassisted walking, is far messier and more exhausting. The sheer amount of curiosity, infantilizing, and hostility I encounter when I move close to the ground wears me down.

· · · · ·

Second Beach north of La Push, Quileute Nation, late spring. Faced with a tangle of driftwood between me and low tide, I start clambering. I leverage myself up onto a log thirty feet long. I sit, trace the salt-scoured ridges, swing my legs over, squirm my way to the trunk tossed against the one I'm currently on, lift myself over it. Scoot sideways some more. Reach across a gap, take hold of the polished remnants of a branch, lean my weight onto the next log. The people ahead of me tightrope across this tumble. I do not covet their balance, nor can I imagine their agility. I keep lifting and leveraging, admiring the bone-white wood, the ocean-sculpted root balls—the shapes reminding me of tentacles, lion heads, sunbursts. A middle-aged white woman stops and hovers over me. I brace myself. She smiles, takes off her sunglasses, enthusing, "You're so brave. I just don't know how you do it." Thankfully she doesn't try to hug me. Behind her, teenage boys keep their distance; my skin prickles and burns as their eyes bore through me.

· · · · ·

I find a belonging in the natural world that I rarely experience among humans. Trees don't gawk. Boulders don't call me inspirational. Oceans don't believe that I and my communities might well be better off dead than disabled. Certainly ableism follows me into the forest and onto the beach. Humans impose all the forces of domination—white supremacy, settler colonialism, capitalism, patriarchy, among others—on the more-than-human world. These systems rip people from earth and sky. They disrupt air and water. They shape who has access and who doesn't. They corrode love and belonging.

At the same time, sitting in the woods or at the ocean, I glimpse a world that relishes crookedness, wholeness and brokenness, an explosion of sizes and shapes. In the more-than-human world, my shaky, asymmetrical body is just one among many. I find spaces and relationships neither saturated with nor defined by ableism.

. . . . .

Gale River Trail, unceded ancestral Wabanaki Confederacy territory, midsummer. Not yet at the infamous boulder staircase known as Jacob's Ladder, we—my sweetie, two nondisabled acquaintances, and I—approach our second stream crossing. The narrow wooden bridge doesn't have railings. My companions navigate it without hesitation. I, on the other hand, pause for a long moment. Maybe I can walk across, but I worry that I might trip, tumbling into the current. I contemplate crawling but immediately cringe, imagining how my new friends might respond. I've already slowed them down significantly. I feel embarrassed, conflicted again. The belief system that declares walking vastly superior to sliding and scooting rises inside me. Shame takes hold yet again. But one step out onto the span, and I know I can't push it. I lower myself to hands and knees and crawl. Shoulder leads; hip follows. The pace, rhythm, and familiarity soothe me. My muscles remember the solidity of crawling. I watch the rushing water through gaps in the planks; the motion doesn't threaten my stability when my center of gravity is this close to the ground. Slowly my shame and fear of falling recede.

. . . . .

I wish the fierce and tender song I'm trying to write could be unequivocal. But in reality, I have thoroughly internalized the dominant belief system about walking—ableism lodged both externally in the human world and internally in my own bodymind. Even without nondisabled people gawking and taunting, I judge my body ugly and awkward. I scoot and crawl mostly as a last resort, rather than as a joyful first choice, because I've swallowed the ableist lies. They've settled deep in my gut and disrupt my love of moving close to the ground.

These falsehoods—*burden*, *clumsy*, *better off dead*, *tragic*, *dangerous*, *not fully human*, *childlike*, *worthless*—also reverberate collectively through disability communities. I want to turn for a moment to disabled and chronically ill people and ask: Given the access, intimacy, and beauty created by moving close to the ground, why don't we talk to each other about these modes of mobility? What are the connections between our internalized ableism and our silence? What do we need to begin this conversation about the joys, embarrassments, dangers, comforts and discomforts, utility, inefficiencies, and access that accompany crawling and scooting?

Surrounding these tender questions is a larger query that I want to ask everyone—disabled and nondisabled, walkie and not—because the ableist beliefs about walking reverberate through all of us in some fashion or another. What do we need to dismantle these beliefs that many of us teach, practice, implement, and enforce in multiple ways? I bring longing and curiosity to these questions.

I've often found my way out of isolation through poetry, music, art, and story. This time I turn to film. I watch Gregor Wolbring, an ability studies scholar and bioethicist, in the documentary *Fixed: The Science/Fiction of Human Enhancement*. With a rebellious glint in his eyes, he claims, "Crawling is in, walking is out." The camera follows Wolbring as he moves through his life—in his home, at an airport, around his lab—mixing different forms of mobility, sometimes using a wheelchair and other times crawling. He says, "I . . . love crawling. . . . I crawl wherever I can." Watching him, I feel just how much my internalized ableism shapes when and where I move on my hands and knees. I aspire to be as rebellious and matter-of-fact as Wolbring.

· · · · ·

Long Trail south of Mt. Abe, unceded ancestral Abenaki territory, early summer. I scoot down a steep tumble of rock. Spots of gray-green lichen prickle my hands. I become an inchworm, humping along. Butt lifts; body weight shifts; knees bend, the glacier-etched schist ridged and warm beneath me.

· · · · ·

I dream plentiful disability-centered conversations about crawling—love songs, manifestos, guidebooks written by a multitude of disabled people who know and claim the joys and discomforts of moving close to the ground. I need layers of stories and politics to undo the ableist belief system about walking embedded in my bodymind, to make space for shunned modes of mobility, and to continue the work of resisting shame. But beyond words, I yearn to scoot, slide, and crawl with other disabled people; to share in community the pleasure and connection I find when I move close to the ground through the woods.

. . . . .

Gale River Trail, unceded ancestral Wabanaki Confederacy territory, midsummer. We arrive at Jacob's Ladder—one thousand feet of elevation gain in less than a mile. I look up at this daunting stretch of trail, granite rocks stairstepping up the mountain. To keep my balance as I climb, I bend slightly at the waist and place my hands three steps above me, a quadruped once again. I slow, feel the skin of boulder against skin of palm. I turn aside repeatedly, giving other hikers the space to pass. I can't move any faster. I breathe the green humid air, settle into this particular rhythm of hands and feet, heart and lungs.

Several years earlier a group of disabled people—three wheelchair users and two crutch users—along with a bunch of nondisabled companions and assistants hiked this trail up to the newly renovated and disability-accessible Galehead Hut. I learned about their adventure from afar, reading about it on the internet. When they reached Jacob's Ladder, Craig Gray slid out of his wheelchair onto the stone stairs and climbed using a move he calls "butt-up." Nicole Haley started singing "You've Lost That Loving Feeling." The whole group urged each other on: "Let's eat that rock."

Across the years, I can almost feel them. My quadruped rhythm merges with Craig's as he leverages his body weight from one step to the next. I hear their encouragements and Nicole's soprano voice belting out the lyrics. I imagine them teasing each other and laughing together as they problem solve. I swear I can feel their pounding hearts.

II

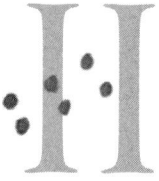

Survivals and Sorrows

CONTENT NOTES: This section is dense with survival and sorrow. Interwoven with release, relief, and individual and communal resistance are:

— references to death, childhood and ritual abuse, disassociation, suicidal thoughts, flashbacks, auditory hallucinations, mass shootings, climate chaos, and early AIDS-epidemic conditions;
— single brief mentions of bullying and dangerous conditions for refugees;
— and impacts of settler colonialism, racism, ableism, and homophobia.

Ruptures

FORMAT NOTE: *Each of the three sections begins with a cluster of lines anchored to the right margin. Midway through the first section, a single sentence fractures, cracking diagonally down the page. At the end of the third section, sentences rupture again in the same way.*

I.

tell it   as a flinch   fracture

tornado   touching down

Early, early, I discovered the art of floating free. Disappearing into roots, rocks, motes of sun. A loosening of time-space-reality. I vanished.

. . . . .

Rupture learned through brutality: This telling requires no details, except to name the ritual abuse group into which I was born. A cluster of survivors turned perpetrators, cycling through four generations (maybe more) in my father's family. Torture passed down from great-grandfather to grandfather; from grandfather, grandmother, great-uncles to father and uncle; from father and uncle to me.

Inheritance locked into tissue, tendon, synapse, aftermath still gripping hard. And yet I did not become a perpetrator.

. . . . .

To disassociate is to

      sever

           split

                refuse association

with bodymind, with self, with pain and terror.

Many ruptures thread through my survival, disassociation only one of them. I rupture from sexual, physical, spiritual terrorizing and mind control. From the unbearable acts my perpetrators trained me to commit. From my childhood home—tree and beach, rock and river.   Flee.   From my disassociated father, a survivor-perpetrator who loved me and broke me. From my complicit mother, full of denial and dismissal. From the hallucinations that taunt and shame me, demand that I return or kill myself.

If I could, I would leave all the violence behind. Shake off the flashbacks, the numbness, the hypervigilance, the many skills gained through survival.

Rewind my life, my father's and uncle's lives, grandmother's and grandfather's lives. Back and back until I found the generation where it started. Then back one more.

Except I cannot return to the past: some long-ago fantasy before cruelty coiled into my family's bones.

2.

tell it   as an uprising of ghosts

barbed wire   puncturing skin   plow

ripping up   big bluestem

Intertwined with this multigenerational cycle of survivors turned perpetrators lies my family's whiteness. My ancestors immigrated to the United States from Norway, Sweden, Ireland, and Scotland by way of Ontario and Manitoba. Farmers looking for land, they arrived in Očhéthi Šakówiŋ (also known now as North Dakota).

In 1890 my great-grandfather's brother took ownership of 160 acres via the 1862 Homestead Act—federal legislation authorizing the US government to give homesteaders free parcels of land. The rolling prairie that my great-granduncle claimed as his property between E-ta-zi-po-ka-se Wakpa (James River) and Sha-i-e-na Ozupi Wakpa (Sheyenne River) had been Sisseton-Wahpeton Dakota homeland.   Still is.   Ceded in 1872–73 under conditions of starvation, bribery, and outright lies.

By 1900 my great-grandparents occupied many acres, slowly paying down a mortgage: already a trail of deeds and money, ink on paper. Homelands of the Pembina band of the Anishinaabeg, ceded in 1863 through a fraudulent treaty with the United States.

And in 1910 my other set of paternal great-grandparents owned a farm outright. That word *owned* pierces me   a deep puncture. They *owned* the land. More Sisseton-Wahpeton Dakota territory.

Thieves, all of them.

Except my ancestors didn't do the actual stealing of land from Indigenous peoples of Očhéthi Šakówiŋ. Rather, the US government massacred, manipulated, starved people. Repeatedly lied as it took possession of Native homelands. Gave them away in turn to non-Native people.

More accurately, my ancestors occupied stolen land as they settled on the western edge of tallgrass prairie, putting into practice white ownership. They divided the land. Established borders and boundaries. Dug postholes and strung barbed wire. Plowed up tallgrass. Put livestock out to graze. As occupiers, they became essential to a system intent on the erasure of Native nations and peoples.

Their individual actions occurred inside entrenched state violence. 1890—my great-granduncle Thomas homesteading in LaMoure County: The US Army massacred hundreds of Lakota people at Wounded Knee.

1900—my great-grandparents Daniel and Eunice hitching oxen to their steel plow: Settlers and government agents had already slaughtered sixty million bison, the great herds nearly extinct. A thundering absence surrounded Daniel and Eunice.

1910—my great-grandparents John and Caroline claiming home on their farm in Cass County: Bureaucrats from the Office of Indian Affairs tore Indigenous families apart. The federal government committed more than a hundred Native people from Očhéthi Šakówiŋ to its Canton Asylum for Insane Indians three hundred miles to the south. Removed thousands of children to boarding schools near and far.

Undoubtedly Thomas-Daniel-Eunice-John-Caroline believed—like most settlers, farmers, business people, US government bureaucrats, and politicians—the lies that Native peoples were vanishing and vanished savages. As occupiers, they refused   ruptured from   the truths of Indigenous personhood, survivance, and kin.

Their violence and ruptures became as common as their own breath.

3.

tell it as wound   still

weeping   callous worn smooth

a slow seep   of truth

My ancestors ruptured from their European homelands. From the Pembina, Sisseton-Wahpeton Dakota, Yanktonai, Mdewakanton. From the destruction and heartbreak they caused. From the impact of greed, occupation, landownership. From the prairie grasses and wide blue sky.

Rupture   upon   rupture.

I feel Thomas-Daniel-Eunice-John-Caroline in my bones. Survivor-perpetrator-occupiers.   Numbnumbnumb,   I start to float free of my bodymind.

They learned rupturing.

      Taught rupturing.

            Practiced rupturing.

                  Strengthened rupturing.

                        Spun rupturing deep into their bodyminds.

I live with their ruptures, and my own, every day. They quiver under my skin.

Flashback

FORMAT NOTE: *Pairs of lines descend diagonally down the page until a single word leaps to the right margin, scattering. The poem then returns to the left margin.*

memory bends
kingfishers dip   below surface

ghosts skim   into air
current   undercuts far bank

reflection blurs   blurs again
slivers everywhere

scatter

and when self
returns
to self

stone   eddy   glint of sun

Hallucinations

FORMAT NOTE: *Toward the end of the poem, several lines stretch horizontally and vertically, dragging across the page.*

They arrived
in mid-July as usual,
voices thundering
into my head—I, living alone
that summer, a half hour
from town, no car,

just a dog, trike,
vegetable garden
out back—
they infiltrated

my inner ear, eye
socket, those tiny
delicate bones
overtaken,

drumbeat
and blur,
I slept

on the screened-in porch,
overlooking cow pastures,
made deals not to leave
the yard without my dog,
and kept plotting to kill myself,

huddled on the kitchen floor
at 4 a.m., no vodka,

time spiked

        dragged

              stalled

                     days into weeks,

and I
survived,

but not
victory,

just
a lonely slog
through
knee-deep
mud.

FORMAT NOTE: *Surrounded by expansive space on the page—words pausing—spare lines float in the lower right corner.*

pause   pause

wild   and quiet

none of us disposable

Love Notes

FORMAT NOTE: *Early in the poem, time slants down the page, three lines descending diagonally toward the right margin. Then the piece springs back to the left margin.*

We may not survive
the decade, much less century. Yet

when deluge descends
this time
          and this time
                    and this time,
surface erupting
in silver fury,

we invite each other down
to the murky bottom.

Fill our ears, throats, bellies
with the stories we most need.

Swim among sunken trees and drowned
rivers, join the loons, dive for our next meal,
find love notes buried in the muck.

Lean Close

FORMAT NOTE: *Two kinds of invitations interspersed: On the left, clusters of lines invite us to lean close to the more-than-human world. Farther right, other clusters invite transformation—skin, bone, voice becoming.*

love sugar maple
white pine
paper birch

lean close
smell their rough
and ruffled skin

        become
        the honey-lit spruce
        of a fiddle fine grained
        and singing

fall
fall
fall in love
often

love creek   cattail
quagmire   love

Superfund site
clear-cut   quarry
third-growth forest

        become
        copper and zinc
        eons before
        they're spun together
        moaning inside
        a saxophone

love the dirt
beneath our feet

bat   bear   bee
on the brink

        become
        long soprano
        notes gusting   gusting
        as the wildfires burn

lungs strain
bellies contract

hearts already
broken   and braced
to break   break
break again

Wail

FORMAT NOTE: *Wailing voices: On the left, places and moments. Anchored to the right margin and italicized, embodied experiences.*

dirt road at 3 a.m.
after a mob boss
snags the presidency

wind rattles against breastbone

. . . . .

planet swinging round
the sun   while sap rises

and refugees trudge
through snow   crust
breaking with each step

history crackles underground

. . . . .

Black church   gay bar
first-grade classroom   just before
a gunman opens fire

aquifers seep through us
time pauses

. . . . .

wail and wail again

FORMAT NOTE: *Surrounded by expansive space on the page—words pausing—spare lines float in the lower right corner.*

pause   pause

sun warms skin

Fleeing

in the years before
I chose queer
but after the bullies
taunted *lezzie*,

before
I remembered
my father's fists but after
my body stored them away,

before
peace demos,
collective houses,
my first kiss,

I knew
I had to leave
that narrow river valley,

Chinook salmon and gun metal,
the people who loved my father
and those who did not.

The Trapdoor of Time

> [My abusers] kept me from telling anyone what was happening to me, but they didn't make me into a torturer.... I understood the first step in becoming like them was to learn to dehumanize others.... Part of the way I prevented this was to envision my abusers as young children, before they became this cruel. I would imagine that imprisoned within the adult bodies that hurt me were captive children who had themselves been tortured.... I imagined how horrified they had to be at the actions of their grown-up selves.
>
> —Aurora Levins Morales, "Torturers"

Your terrorizing no longer rules my life. I haven't seen or talked to you for more than twenty years. Inside this gift of estrangement, I repeatedly fantasize your death. Wait for it. Yearn for it. And then it actually happens.

You die. Alone in your bed. Of dementia.

Time ruptures. I revisit the violence seeped into every corner of every room we lived in together. Memory piles upon memory—jumbled time, survivor time, grief time. But not sorrow time.

For months after your last breath, pine, hemlock, cedar comfort me. I discover anew that inside your violence and ownership of my bodymind hovers a deep fierce gentle love.

I am eight, twelve, seventeen, fifty-five, eighty-three, not yet born. In dozens of ways, you advocate for me—your spastic, hard-to-understand, first-born child. You protect me from bullies. Tromping through second-growth forest, you teach me alder and tan oak. Hunkering down at tide pools, you show me anemone and hermit crab. Working in your woodshop, you encourage me to use hand plane and jigsaw. As strangers stare at my tremoring hands, you insist: *Their problem, not yours.* You introduce me to the ideas of Thomas Jefferson, Winston Churchill, Ayn Rand. I am eight, twelve, seventeen, fifty-five, eighty-three, not yet born, and I too love you. At every juncture, you harm me in unbearable ways that I learn to bear.

Time bends around your bewildering love. It brings me to my knees. You never stop being a right-wing, cruel, angry, unpredictable, alcoholic perpetrator.

This story told not in words but slivers and hangovers: I piece it together. You survive prolonged family violence. Attempt to escape. Fail. Continue in the multigenerational tradition of survivors turned perpetrators.

You lead me deep into that legacy. But again fail. I flee. Grief time nourishes sorrow only for who you might have been.

I listen for your survivor's love in my heart. Find your obituary. It tells lies in all the predictable ways. On Facebook, your former students and coworkers gush—an outpouring of gratitude. They declare you a mentor, the best teacher they ever had, a smart and funny friend.

Time wavers.

I do not attend your memorial service. Nor do I know where your second wife and stepchildren, along with my siblings, scatter your ashes. Grief time cradles no sorrow for the man you actually became but also no glee for your death.

Time warps.

I search for the death announcements of the men who shaped the multigenerational ritual abuse network you were born into and the one you found in rural Oregon. Grandfather, uncle, landlord, dairy farmer, sixth-grade teacher: all dead. This knowledge seeps through me, every single cell of my bodymind thirsty. Those men will never harm me again. I feel relief but no joy.

Still. Still. Still.

The trapdoor of time swings wide. I tumble into the chasm and keep tumbling. Not flashback or hallucination, nighttime terror or dissociative fugue, time itself ruptures. I lose my place. I don't know which hour of what day holds me, which day of what week nor what month of which season. Nothing anchors me. I try to find myself on a calendar, but the boxes simply dip and wheel.

Time spirals.

I land at the confluence, earth meeting river meeting lake. I thank the water, the sun not quite set, the Abenaki people past-present-future. I listen again for your love.

Time bunches.

I catch flickers across the river. Squint. And see you—my father at six years old, a skinny, scrappy boy—climbing in the driftwood that washes downstream in flash floods and spring freshets.

Time whispers and echoes.

You grow up on a dirt farm in Očhéthi Šakówiŋ (known to you as North Dakota), near the settler town of Barnes, one of three children—your brother, a cousin, and you—in a multigenerational household of nine. You all scrape through the Great Depression and the Dust Bowl. Plow fields, milk cows, hoe vegetable gardens, collect chicken eggs. Your mother cleans offices in Barnes;

your father digs graves. Already at six, you are a survivor; ritual abuse loops and howls beneath your skin.

A white boy hunting rabbits on the railroad beds and old wagon tracks, you fall in love with the wide horizon and swallow the lies of the settler colonial nation-state and patriarchy. You have no clue about the starvation, resistance, and day-to-day life of the Sisseton-Wahpeton Dakota on the Lake Traverse Reservation a hundred miles due south. You don't know that your entire family—grandparents and granduncles and grandaunts, your parents and their siblings, your cousins, everyone, yourself included—occupies stolen Indigenous land, your home made possible by pure thievery and massacre. They raise you in a legacy of rupture and silence. Your ignorance redeems nothing. Slowly you learn cruelty.

Time skips.

Newly married and awaiting your first child, you move across the continent to the south coast of Oregon, unceded homeland of the Quatomah band of the Tututni people. Weekends you wander the beaches at low tide, climbing in the mountains of driftwood at the mouth of Elk River. The long horizon reminds you of the prairies. Weekdays you teach US history to teenagers.

You fill your classroom with lessons about dead white men and the brilliance of their version of democracy. Your lectures transform Indigenous people into violent savages intent on stopping settlers' westward migration. Transform the enslavement of Black people into a tale of states' rights. Transform the New Deal into a communist plot. When you lose your temper, you hurl blackboard erasers, bouncing them off the back wall.

I learn a million lies from you; they tunnel into me. Across many years and thousands of miles, I wrench myself free.

Time trembles.

At the confluence, I squint again. You flicker: a little boy dancing and squealing, engrossed in wood, water, sand. Flicker: you, a survivor-perpetrator-occupier learning the lessons deeply, teaching them relentlessly. Your legacy and mine. I listen.

Time splinters.

Current meets current. In this moment, I am not afraid.

Warm Breathing Space

FORMAT NOTE: *This poem interweaves distilled images of body anchored to the right with long lines of memory anchored to the left.*

Between liver and lung,
belly and hunger:

I used to squeeze beneath the bed. Count creaks, spasms, my parents' foot-steps. Briefest of moments: no one prying me open.

Between synapse and bone, tendril
of nerve and hunch of pain:

Crawl deep into the hay barn. Burrow among the bales to find warm breathing space.

Between riverbed and boulder,
thunder and drenching rain:

I never imagined the day I would climb into the wild blue open, no longer alone.

Fifty Years After He Beat Me

Hinge where pelvis
meets spine—tender, tender:

bones radiate
heat until the golden tips

of his cowboy boots,
lodged in rib and hip,

shimmer out of me,
gold never meant

as weapon
or wound: they twirl

into meteorites
streaking across the sky.

The Art of Disassociation

FORMAT NOTE: *Short—often one word—lines descend in a steep arc, flying toward the right edge of the page. Interspersed into this arc are pairs of lines anchored to the left margin.*

drift

lose time   gain time
ride the time machine

spin

shred the diagnoses
into sheer   survival

fly

watch them rain down
like pride parade confetti

vanish

claim ourselves
escape artists

efficient and beautiful

FORMAT NOTE: *Surrounded by expansive space on the page—words pausing—spare lines float in the lower right corner.*

pause   pause

steel guitar glints

Aretha and Sister Rosetta rising

in feet   hips   shoulders

a dappling of joy

A Murmuration of Survival

HISTORICAL NOTE: *This poem swirls through (and beyond) the early AIDS epidemic before effective life-saving drugs existed. Those years (1981–95) felt like an eternity of funerals. I remember the first unfolding of the AIDS Memorial Quilt, nearly two thousand panels stretching out over a hundred yards on the National Mall, Washington, DC, in 1987. I remember how most people of all genders with HIV/AIDS were demonized and treated as utterly disposable. I remember medical and religious hatred, governmental silence and denial. I remember people with AIDS (PWAs) taking care of each other and lesbians and gay men coming together to tend to the living and the dying. The first antiretroviral medications that saved the lives of PWAs became widely available in 1996. They made a huge difference for people who had health insurance or could otherwise afford them.*

FORMAT NOTE: *On the left, years anchor the lived histories that unspool fragmented down the center. On the right, distilled images of survival and sorrow reverberate.*

A cloud of starlings drifts from the river,
at first, a smudge on the sky . . .
then more definite,

contracting then scattering
like pain.
  —Jake Adam York, "A Murmuration of Starlings"

1983:   we drink   and smoke
                 that dive on Telegraph
                 Ave   resolve to dance
                 cruise   play pool

                 mob bosses   no longer
                 rule the bars   but

                 inevitably   last week's
                 funerals overtake us

                                                  our tears

2016:   putting water on
to boil   NPR chatters
in the background

then sudden   words
catch   like rapping
on the window—

gunman   gay bar   Pulse
2 a.m.   forty-nine dead—reporter's
voice   smooth   steady

                                               a cupful of tea

1983:   this epidemic   barely
named   but the dead   already
echo   through bedrooms
alleyways   late-night   phone calls

1988:   our voices   press
together—*act up*
fight back   fight AIDS

2016:   as if   just another
news story   smell
floods the room

1983:   alcohol   sweat
urine on concrete

                                         a fistful of glitter

2016:   morning sun dapples
the kitchen   touch floorboard
joist   cellar wall   touch

breastbone   touch
belly   but inside

this smell
no way
out

                                                    an ocean of rage

1983:   at 1 a.m.   teenage
             white boys

             lurk   in anticipation
             hurling slurs

                                                    a pride of comets

1988:   someone up ahead   a cloud
             of bodies   denim jacket
             painted   thick white letters
             atop a pink triangle

             IF I DIE OF
             AIDS — FORGET
             BURIAL — JUST
             DROP MY BODY
             ON THE STEPS
             OF THE F.D.A.

                                          a galaxy of what-ifs and farewells

1994:   some of us   you   and
             you   and you   return
             to your childhood
             homes   because

             death   slinks everywhere
             no one remaining   to feed you
             warm broth   change
             your sheets

2020:   too familiar   the bodies
                 stack up   outside
                 the morgues

1983/1988/1994/ do not ask
2016/2020:   how many
                 we cannot
                 keep count

                                          swoop and dive

2022:   wake up   news   yet
                 another massacre
                 this time—Club Q

                 drop our bodies
                 on the steps
                 of the NRA

1983/1988/1994/ names   obituaries
2016/2020/2022: funerals—swirling flocks
                 of songbirds

1983:   we close the bar   escort
                 one another to our cars
                 the late-night bus

                 skin salty   eyes blurry   we
                 belt out Gloria Gaynor
                 Donna Summer

                                    a murmuration of survival

III

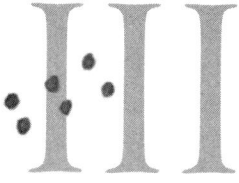

Moving Toward Porousness

CONTENT NOTES: This section interweaves belonging and community with references to death and impacts of ableism, homophobia, the gender binary, transphobia, enslavement of Black people, and settler colonialism.

Midair

branching river
of beech roots, crow feather

ruffled and bent,
shower of hemlock cones,

fleck of feldspar,
swoop of suspension

cables, bridge
floating midair

follow the fractures and fault lines.

Creating Categories

In the one-room public library of my childhood, I start taking baby steps toward queerness, drenched in teenage confusion and questions. I search for myself in books. I've read my way through the Hardy Boys and Nancy Drew mysteries, migrating over the years to adult fiction and nonfiction. I practice looking up my favorite subjects in the library catalog, flipping through the drawers of index cards organized alphabetically by Dewey decimal subject headings. (In 1979, Google, desktop computers, and digital library catalogs did not exist yet.) I adore the process of searching for books and knowledge. So I turn again to the card catalog to try to make sense of the turmoil in my head and heart, furtively looking up the subject *Homosexuality*. I pull a single volume off the shelf, sit on the floor, read the words *deviant, pervert, immoral*.

Now, decades later, I still browse libraries. Walking in the stacks, I often think about categories. Whether queer/trans youth discover vibrant LGBTQ books in their public library or newly disabled people find books that open the door into disability culture depends partly on subject headings and keywords. If they are assigned in one way, we're likely to encounter pathology, and in another way, the possibility of connection and community. The details of cataloging books are not as innocuous as they appear at first glance.

. . . . .

Classification systems exert tremendous power. They define and maintain hierarchies of categories used to describe and understand objects and beings—human and more-than-human, organic and inorganic. These systems often appear unassailable, and the people who create and employ them are often more inclined to bend what they are categorizing to fit their categories than vice versa.

I want to think about the power of categorization by examining the Library of Congress (LOC) subject headings. At first glance, this exploration may seem a bit absurd. The classifying of books holds so little power over people's lives compared to other systems of classification—the gender binary or diagnostic categorization as laid out in the *Diagnostic and Statistical Manual of Mental Disorders* (DSM) and the International Classification of Diseases, for instance. Yet the ways in which the LOC system interlocks with diagnosis, gender, and settler colonial nationhood reveal much about how classification systems in general build and maintain authority.

As I flipped through the card catalog searching for *homosexuality*, I had no idea that someday I would be a published writer, my books assigned subject headings and call numbers and shelved in libraries across the country. I think of the LOC headings assigned to my first book. They read, "1. Clare, Eli. 2. Women political activists—United States—Biography. 3. Cerebral palsied—United States—Biography." In 1999 holding the newly published *Exile and Pride: Disability, Queerness, and Liberation* in my hands, I remember glancing at the copyright page and skimming the subject headings. I grumpily thought, "Wait! Those words don't describe the book I wrote." But quickly I resigned myself, believing somehow that those categories were immutable.

Now though, I want to focus more closely on some of these headings, in particular, *Cerebral palsied*, *Women*, and *United States*. I'll start with *Cerebral palsied*. This descriptor places me and my book in relationship to diagnosis. The medical-industrial complex would have us believe that diagnosis is a universal, capital-T Truth, supposedly infallible, except when misdiagnosis has occurred. In this situation, we are told simply to wait for the correct diagnosis to emerge. But for a moment, I want to consider diagnosis as just another system of classification, and *cerebral palsy* as a single category within that system. As such, diagnosis defines and names bodymind conditions deemed pathological, charting a network of connections between them. Sometimes it provides us access to vital medical technology and treatment, and other times it pathologizes our entire beings. All too often it is brandished as authority, our bodyminds bent to match diagnostic criteria rather than vice versa. As a system of classification, diagnosis shapes many kinds of interactions in doctors' offices and emergency rooms, research labs and public health think tanks. At the same time, its authority to name, describe, and define pathology extends far beyond those medical spaces, reaching into the LOC subject headings, which include the descriptor *cerebral palsied*.

This adjective links me and my book to diagnosis rather than to my self-chosen and politicized identity of disabled. I relish my connections with disabled, d/Deaf, chronically ill, Mad, and neurodivergent peoples. Unequivocally I identify as a disabled person. Having cerebral palsy is no secret in my life. Yet the LOC's choice of that diagnosis turned subject heading utterly disregards the ways I claim myself and hands the power of naming bodyminds over to the medical-industrial complex.

Let me turn now to *Women* in the headings assigned to *Exile and Pride*. It, too, is used as a descriptor and locates me and my book in relationship to the gender binary. In the current dominant version of this classification system, two categories exist: *female-feminine-woman* and *male-masculine-man*. Into these two predetermined options, the gender binary tries to corral the thousands of ways humans combine hormones; grow hair, curves, muscles, genitals, and reproductive organs; adorn our bodyminds; find pleasure; understand and name our sexed and gendered selves. By design, this hierarchal system values men over women, attempts to erase the existence of transgender and nonbinary people, and frequently punishes transgression and variation.

As a classification scheme and system of power, the gender binary never functions in isolation. For example, diagnosis interlocks with and polices the binary in intense ways, pathologizing people whose genders and sexes don't conform. I think of how *congenital general hypertrichosis* pathologizes bearded women, how *testicular hypofunction* pathologizes beardless men, and how a whole raft of diagnoses under the umbrella of *disorders of sex development* pathologize intersex people whose bodyminds don't match medicalized definitions of female and male. Certainly the diagnostic process sometimes helps individual people in a variety of sexed and gendered struggles. But on a systemic level, diagnosis as a classification scheme functions to undergird, gatekeep, and authorize the binary. It joins with other systems of power—patriarchy, white supremacy, capitalism, ableism, and on and on—all of them interlocking to make *woman* and *man* appear overwhelmingly natural, scientific, and unquestionable.

In using *Women* as a descriptor in the subject heading *Women political activists*, the LOC piggybacks on this intertwined set of systems. The heading is of course authorized by the binary. But additionally it is bolstered by the interlocking of diagnostic, racial, settler colonial, and sexual orientation categorization schemes, among many others. At the same time, the LOC's gendered headings aren't only *reinforced* through these schemes; they also play a role in *reinforcing* them. This entire network of mutually reinforced and reinforcing systems creates a facade of unyielding authority.

Within this facade, the descriptor *women* assigned to *Exile and Pride* makes invisible the expansive queer and transgender frameworks I call home. Without a doubt, being a girl/woman for more than three decades before medically and socially transitioning to live in the world as a white guy has totally shaped my work. But slotting my book into the binary distorts who I am and how I write about the tangle of gender, both in my life and the world around me.

And now, finally, let me turn to *United States*. Unlike *Cerebral palsied* and *Women*, this subject heading doesn't originate in another classification system. Rather, it is known in the LOC system as a "geographic component," which functions to name a land-based place connected neither to an author's location or citizenship but to the geography of a book's content. This feature seems innocuous enough, except it relies almost exclusively on nation-state borders and names. *United States* is not simply a land-based place but also a location of power and domination—a settler colonial political entity made possible by land stolen from Indigenous peoples and labor coerced from enslaved Black people.

The subject heading *United States* locates me and my words inside a violent nation-state rather than an ecosystem or bioregion. *United States* makes invisible the thievery of the Indigenous land that I grew up on as a white settler. That land—the unceded homeland of the Quatomah band of the Tututni people—is central to the themes of *Exile and Pride*. *United States* can never simply be a descriptive location, not the same as, for example, the imagined subject heading *Watershed of the Kusuma (Elk River)*. Instead, *United States* subsumes my work into a power structure and political entity that I've struggled against, as both a writer and an activist, most of my adult life.

All of these subject headings—*Cerebral palsied*, *Women*, and *United States*—claim me and my work in ways I would never claim myself. For years, they irritated me but at the same time seemed beyond question. I had swallowed the lie that these LOC categories and this classification system as a whole are irrefutable. So many categorization schemes maintain their power precisely because they appear indisputable.

. . . . .

A decade and a half after first holding *Exile and Pride* in my hands, I receive an email from my friend Madeline Veitch, who works as a university librarian. She tells me that while cataloging my book, she has been struck by its subject headings. She observes that "headings around queer and disability activism and communities are abysmal. I just went looking for a heading for 'disability activists,' and it does not exist." She suggests adding three new categories to the bibliographic record for my book. Her words excite me, but I can barely keep up as she lays out the details. She asks for feedback on her suggestions: *Gender identity*, *Transgender people—Biography*, and *People with disabilities—Biography*. All three are official LOC headings, entering the system in different years (1991 for *Gender identity*, 2007 for *Transgender*, and 2002 for the change from *Handicapped* to *People with disabilities*).

Madeline knows that the LOC made this classification system up and that, in turn, it can be revised. She also understands the power she wields in assigning these categories. She tells me about the headings she wants to petition the LOC to create, starting with *Disability activists*. "There are so many . . . I'd like to add that don't exist, like 'intersections of identity' and 'genderqueer people.'"

We end up in an extended email conversation about the ways in which diagnosis and pathology hinge into all kinds of subject headings. For instance, the LOC considers both *AIDS (Disease)—Patients* and *Cancer—Patients* preferred headings, turning some bodymind conditions into diagnoses and diseases, and people with those particular conditions into patients. The LOC could use the less medicalized and more community-based language of *People with AIDS/HIV* and *Cancer survivors* just as it could use a more expansive gender system to tag authors and subject matter, and bioregions or Indigenous nations and place names to geographically locate books. Instead it has created a system that both relies on and reinforces diagnostic language and concepts, the gender binary, and settler colonial nation-states.

These interlocking systems appear unassailable but turn out to be entirely contingent. Indigenous people continue the work of decolonizing their homelands and nations. Native librarians create book classification systems that decenter settler colonial nation-states. Transgender, gender nonconforming, and genderqueer people expand the binary. Activists work to depathologize LGBTQ people, successfully campaigning forty years ago to remove *homosexuality* from the *DSM*. Hate-filled language like *mental retardation* changes slowly, disabled people choosing *intellectually disabled*, *self-advocate*, *neurodivergent*, and that language filtering into classification schemes. So many of us are working to unravel the authority of these systems.

Recently Madeline and I picked our conversation back up. She writes, "In the years since we [last] spoke, . . . I stopped believing I could succeed with [subject] heading proposals, before I even began. . . . I think I was naive at the time. That said, I talked with [a colleague] about it recently and he was like, 'it can be done, you could do it.' So maybe I just lost faith in my own agency and should work to regain it." As I read her words, my heart hurts. To retain their authority, the systems of power that create, maintain, and gatekeep these classification schemes count on us becoming disillusioned. I write back, "Madeline, in the long-haul work of reshaping categories and questioning their authority, we need hope; we need the naiveté that allows us to be audacious; we need tenacity informed by both impatience and an understanding of how slow and grinding change often is."

I long for categories that no longer function as tools of social control but instead bend to match what they sort, define, and name. I want us—naive, hopeful, disillusioned, committed to the long haul—to reshape current classification schemes and build brand new ones: responsive, flexible, insistent on multiplicity. Yet in spite of our best efforts, every category we invent will inevitably end up excluding/misnaming someone or something. So in our creating, we need to center the marginalized, the quirky, the in-between, the porous. And maybe in this process, the very act of categorization will completely transform.

In-Between

FORMAT NOTE: *The dream at the heart of this poem floats italicized in the center of the page.*

The world between
sleep and wake: untethered
from time and space,
trees and rocks whisper:

> *a quilt   the yellow-green*
> *of beech   and birch in autumn*
> *unfolds   part wood   part cloth*
> *a grand   stringed instrument*
> *long   alto notes   vibrate*
> *among the trees*

I float, warm
and loose limbed,
tremors everywhere.

Turning Away from Categories

I.

In disability communities, we sometimes talk about the diagnoses that we use to name our bodyminds or that doctors assign to us. But we're more inclined to pass information about successful access hacks, tell sweet stories about first dates, and exchange pain-management strategies. We aren't so much unmaking diagnostic categories as turning away from them for the moment. Some of us will return, for many different reasons, to those categories. But in community, even as shared or differing diagnoses can point us toward deeper understandings of our bodyminds, they only form one small part of the connective tissue between us.

2.

Portland, Oregon, 2010: I'm facilitating a disability writing workshop, happy to see a disabled friend from trans community across the table. The room fills with familiar chaos as ten of us negotiate two dozen different kinds of needs—food, breaks, furniture arrangements. We move slowly. Creating access takes priority.

Several people have requested PAs (personal assistants) beforehand. One of them doesn't show up. I watch my friend hesitate. Without a PA, he is left needing a scribe. As a group, we decide I'll slide into that role. I give everyone the first prompt, then drag my chair close to his, pull out my laptop.

· · · · ·

I worry this venture will fail. I type with one finger—halting, shaky, and above all else slow. Needless to say, I am never anyone's first choice as scribe. We start: You speak, and I type, my hands shaking, shoulders tight as I try to keep pace with your words. You pause. I apologize for slowing you down. You look at me, say, "No. I like seeing your finger jerking key to key."

We continue. I begin to feel a rhythm. Your speech halts and flutters as you search for the right images. Still I believe my slowness must be hindering you. I check in. Again you say, "No." And then: "I rarely get to see my tremors reflected in someone else's."

I feel your eyes brush my hands. Your gaze doesn't tug, burn, bore, assess, demand, taunt. It doesn't define, name, devalue. It has no relationship to *normal* or *abnormal*, to diagnosis or pathology, treatment or cure. Rather, your eyes invite me to be right here, right now.

Your Breath in the Pixels

HISTORICAL NOTE: *Self-advocate, artist, writer, and philosopher Mel Baggs died at age thirty-nine in April 2020. One of hir lasting legacies is hundreds of posts spread over at least six separate blogs and Tumblrs, a dozen or more YouTube videos, and a substantial handful of published articles and interviews.*

FORMAT NOTE: *Mel Baggs's italicized words begin and end this piece. Between the two, my imagined dialogue with hir unfolds—my voice on the left, hirs on the right, alternating.*

Came from the redwoods, which tell me who I am and where I belong in the world. . . .

    . . . the rocks, the slugs, the dirt, the trees, and the fungus seemed to have no problem with being in the same world as me, and letting me know in so many ways that I belonged there. It was human beings that shut me out . . .

> *My task here is to scale the cliffs of language and shout up to you the pattern of one or more injustices. . . .*

Words shimmering
across our computer screens:
we never met in person,

even though we made home
in the same watershed.
Lack of access thwarted us.

> *If the powerful people in a society build everything around them, and the powerful people are not wheelchair users, then a wheelchair user will likely face a particular and awful difficulty. We find that no matter where we go, the very structure of the environment excludes us.*

I swallowed
your posts whole,
looped your videos
over and over,

your breath
whispering
through the pixels,

beats and pops
of your refrains
sinking into me.

*Counters are too high, staircases
abound, curbs end abruptly, ramps exist
only in a few places, drinking fountains
remain out of reach, and so on and so
forth. . . . What I most want to talk about,
however, is language. Like counters,
stairs, and drinking fountains, language
was built mostly by non-autistic people,
with the obvious results. . . .*

Your words beckoned,
a torrent chronicling
the forces of erasure

that ripped
through your world,
an everyday undertow.

*My biggest frustration is this: the most
important things about the way I
perceive and interact with the world
around me can only be expressed in
terms that describe them as the absence
of something important.*

I regret
knowing you only
through words:

we never leaned
in to each other

listening to the hush
of white pines, slosh
of lake against rock,

never smelled
books together nor
watched flags flap,

never traded rhythms.

The absence of speech.
The absence of language.
The absence of thought.
The absence of movement.
The absence of comprehension.
The absence of feeling.
The absence of perception. . . .

I never gimped down
the cliffs to join you
in your valley.

I can tap out rhythms in general or
those of my favorite numbers. (I really
like the rhythm of seven, for example.) I
can speak Feline about as well as
anyone with my limited human senses. . . .

I remember: years ago,
word trickling through
disability community—

you languishing in the hospital,
dangerously sick.

Your doctors lied,
blustered, refused
to treat you. We flooded

the switchboard with calls,
until they relented.

*Everything I perceive—from the
movements of my body to the smells in
the air—goes into my mind and sifts
itself into . . . patterns. . . .*

But this time, this time—
your lungs clogged
and desperate—

the news arrived
on a Monday
morning via Facebook:

*I consider these patterns and
connections to be more my language
than the words that appear on the
screen when I let my fingers use the
keyboard. And far more my language
than the words that have popped out of
my mouth throughout my life. They are
how the world makes sense to me.
Anything else is just the artifact of a
shoddy translation. . . .*

You did not survive.
Cause of death—poverty,
isolation, ableism:

                    you

who could have been
a friend.

To me, typical language takes place in the clouds, and I have to climb or fly up there just to use and understand it. This is exhausting no matter how fluent I sound or how easy I make it look.

Both of us
tracing
the pixels.

The sky will always be a foreign country to me. . . . To use my more natural means of communication, I don't have to leave the ground at all.

. . . when I am done with my place in the human world, I will turn into all the animals and fungi and plants and microbes that will likely eat my remains. . . .

I may yet be a redwood tree when I grow up. . . .

When Categories Fail

Sometimes we reshape existing categories, unravel them and create new ones. Or we turn away from their authority in order to claim ourselves and each other on our own terms. But still they exist—organizing, defining, controlling.

. . . . .

I love the places where categories fail spectacularly. Where ocean meets sand —a pounding of water and softening of land. Where current encounters current—a swell at the confluence. Where ecosystem overlaps ecosystem— an overflow of life. In these places, categories bend, strain, break. They can't contain the messiness and plenty.

. . . . .

Beyond the categories and classification schemes, there are portals of connection, understanding, and belonging. We find them. We build them. We imagine them. Porous, flexible, insistent on multiplicity.

We need all the liberatory futures we can possibly dream, but we don't have to wait for these portals to emerge. Many of them already exist.

Unclassifiable

For decades I've named my gendered self a boulder who splits the current and dreams. I adore how unclassifiable this gender is. Settler colonial diagnoses, the LOC subject headings, and the binary simply cannot contain it.

I enter a portal where there are simply too many genders to count, sort, define, much less gatekeep. Here, the shorthand of nonbinary, genderqueer, and gender nonconforming doesn't exist anymore. No longer living in relationship to gendered normalcy and conformity, we've untethered from the binary. Refuse to replace it with some other classification scheme.

Inside this portal, I experience deep gender belonging. I join with others who understand their gender(s) as boulder—that slow steadiness always at the mercy of water and wind. But I also gravitate toward multigender space. Genders run the gamut from feather to stud, woman to punk, cupcake to spiderweb, ripple to man, queen to velvet ruby, femme to infinity, disco ball to heat-rising-off-the-sidewalk. I often taste the sweetness and contentiousness between us as we unlearn gender hierarchy and domination and begin new kinds of solidarity.

. . . . .

June 2024: In this time of rising white nationalism, far-right legislators, and virulent transphobia, my claim that this portal already exists may seem absurd. As trans/nonbinary people (particularly trans youth and trans women/femmes of color), we are struggling hard for survival; for access to health care; for space to be ourselves in schools, on the streets, in our homes. Yet I'm inviting us to live inside a portal we're still building, still dreaming into existence, but at the exact same time already exists right here, right now.

If Only

I'd gladly
forgo
opposable thumbs, entice
fingers into feathers,

if only

to dart
on ruby-throated wings,

      river of dreams
      cold and clear

cast language aside,

if only

to accept
beaver's invitation, she
leading me deep
inside her lodge,

teaching me
to grow
a paddle-shaped tail,

      river of sunlight
      undammed

surrender
my tender human heart,

if only

to share
heron's glee,
standing transfixed
in knee-deep
water, sunrise to sunset,

      river of songs
      river of stardust

if only

to burrow
into the long
slow time
of granite covered
with lichen.

IV

Dreams and Rebellions

CONTENT NOTES: This section interweaves resistance, dreams of liberation, connection, and belonging with:

— references to death, institutionalization, trauma-induced nightmares, and COVID-19 pandemic conditions;
— brief and single mentions of police violence and houselessness;
— and impacts of child abuse, ableism, racism, and fatphobia.

.

Learning to Dream

FORMAT NOTE: *Clusters of lines anchored to the right margin punctuate and distill the prose.*

I.

Floating out of sleep, I reach toward a dream drifting nearby. I sense its color, shape, sound, but the details, though vivid, remain just beyond my fingertips. Bodymind warm, slow, right arm dancing with random tremors, no spasms—by the time I'm actually awake, I barely remember that anything has slipped away. So ordinary, and yet these ephemeral currents still feel unfamiliar.

Dreams slosh
through the world,
climbing over
each other, sliding
underneath.

For my first thirty-five years, I rarely dreamed. In those decades, slumber wrapped me in gummy tendrils. I almost never experienced the quirkiness of ruby-red slippers or the wonder of soaring on an updraft. As a child, I survived endless nights of violence by transforming loops of terror and pain into phantoms, which I then pushed off the edge of my world. I talked gibberish, yelled through walls, walked in my sleep—muscles braced for the next onslaught. But I never swam in the slumber-time currents of image, glimmer, half story.

In other words, I joined a multitude of survivors kidnapped from our dreams. The doors slam hard, locking us away. Deadbolts click into place—keys hidden well with the intent that we will never find them. Flashbacks and nighttime terrors tunnel through our synapses. We lose not just slumber-time currents but also our capacity to imagine, desire, and invent.

In my dreamless twenties, I lived in queer collective households. Mornings at 233 Warwick Avenue just up the hill from Lake Merritt, I often stood in the kitchen, spreading peanut butter on toast, listening to my housemates. They recounted mundane and weird dreams as their first cups of caffeine jolted them into the waking world. I never had anything to add to these conversations.

I couldn't conceive of sleep populated by the fragmented, fantastical encounters they described. Climbing crisscrossing ladders (orange, red, pink) up and up to Mars, swimming through billowy sunset clouds, walking into crystal tunnels that morph into skyscrapers and lecture halls—these encounters shared nothing in common with the small handful of repeating nightmares that punctured my sleep, whirling around my bedroom. Mostly I didn't know if I was awake or not, if the knives cascading around me were real or hallucinations. And then I'd fall back into thick, viscous sleep.

I told my friends to rouse me if ever our house caught fire because otherwise I might not escape. Not just ordinarily deep or heavy, my dreamless sleep numbed me like a drug, a fist, dragging me down, muffling all my internal alarm systems. I feared that I simply wouldn't wake up.

> Dreams clack one
> against another
> as they rock together
> in the shallows, salt water
> meeting sand.

Slowly, slowly I turned to face those violent childhood nights. I started the long-haul bodymind-wrenching process of remembering the unremembered. I slogged through that first decade of work, rattled every day by flashbacks. I learned to recognize and defuse triggers. To release fear. To sit with sorrow. I shook; I cried; I drifted away; I whispered my childhood truths for the first time. Little by little I bound self back to self.

Somewhere amid this process, sleep began to feel less sticky, more like a draught of cool water, a steady stream flowing through me. My reoccurring nightmares diminished. Tendons and ligaments loosened. Dreams arrived without fanfare—mundane, quirky, often dissolving back into the rhythm of my sleep.

These visitations bewildered me—unfamiliar and sometimes downright bizarre. I didn't trust them, convinced they were passing fancies, not to be counted on. Gummy sleep devoid of dreams had so marked my survival and shaped the texture of my days. But much to my surprise, these newfound visitations stuck around. Night after night they worked their way through me. Over time, my suspicion morphed into curiosity. Sleep leavened with dreams became a reclamation.

2.

Dreams emerge as invitation. As emotion. As foretelling. They function as reminder. As release. As revelation. They reflect anxiety and chaos. Reveal desire. Unfold as visits from earth and spirit. Slowly over the years all these permutations have introduced themselves to me.

Dreams invite connection across time and space. A friend I haven't seen in too long, our early pandemic years spent on opposite edges of the continent, appears one night:

> *You skydive into my sleep. I see you in silhouette, sitting in your wheelchair, drifting down through a canopy of maples, hair wild and curly. Delight flashes through me. You, here. But then your parachute doesn't billow open. A moment of panic before I realize the trees will catch you.*

A magic visit across thousands of miles

Dreams crack open joy:

> *Bright tropical tree frogs—reds, oranges, purples, blues, greens more vivid than any language or pigment can actually catch—leap up my leg.*

This radiant image evaporates into the morning light of my bedroom. I feel bereft, caught off guard not by how fantastical this encounter is but by how real. I find a tattooist, ask her to mark my skin with these tiny amphibians and their ephemeral colors—my first tattoo.

Dreams drag me into sorrow:

> *I kayak the river I grew up on. Water flattens into my most familiar swimming hole, fifteen feet deep, rock ledges line one side, opposite bank opens into sandbar, hay pasture, abandoned orchard soaked in sun. I join the salmon fingerlings and mudpuppies, water striders and barn swallows. I take the sharp bends, slow meanders, chattering riffles. Downstream gorse lines both banks; plywood mill, long closed in waking life, still clatters. And suddenly I'm paddling a dry riverbed, boat no longer afloat, water vanished into rock.*

I wake, throat aching, still seeing that bone-dry channel where currents used to rush. All day, I'm haunted by aquifers collapsing, wells running dry, rivers tapering to a trickle.

> Gleaming in the night,
> dreams lay twenty thousand eggs;
> some unfurl into
> the future, others dissolve
> back to sand.

3.

Our sleeping dreams shape muscle memory, carve pathways for the daytime work of conjuring communal thriving. But for many of us—grief piled upon grief, survival upon survival—imagining liberation feels impossible. Capitalism, white supremacy, patriarchy benefit tremendously from our diminished and kidnapped dreams.

I know my justice dreaming too often stays reactive, engaged with an end to violence and shame rather than a proactive creation of joy and freedom. Sometimes all I can conjure is *no*—no to war, no to prisons, no to deportation, no to rape. I sit braced against a wall built from generations of rebellion and noncompliance.

How do we untether from our fear and exhaustion, float toward wild, uncontainable dreaming?

Disabled Puerto Rican Jewish poet and historian Aurora Levins Morales burrows underneath this question. She talks about how our justice dreaming is often dismissed, trivialized as "just utopian." The intent is to shut down the power of desire. These dismissals only serve to maintain the status quo. Her words invite us to actively claim utopian dreaming.

We who long for quirky, queer and trans, disabled and chronically ill, BIPOC futures are in the midst of teaching each other to dream. Both playful and serious, we ask: *What are our superpowers?* This question is intentionally silly, meant to shake loose our imaginations. Sometimes we name skills and knowledges we already have—ones that we need to encourage and value because they will save us. We tell each other:

I repair solar panels and heat pumps.
I grow food.
I dig deep with words.
I find keys and pick dead bolts.
I sew clothes.
I encourage the calming of nervous systems.
I live the brilliance of disabled ingenuity.

But I, the activist-survivor-poet who didn't always have capacity to dream, still filled with reluctance and more *no* than *yes*—how do I wholeheartedly embrace my own justice dreaming?

I turn to the wisdom of Black lesbian feminist mother warrior poet Audre Lorde. She writes, "I speak here of poetry as a revelatory distillation of experience. . . . It forms the quality of the light within which we predicate our hopes and dreams toward survival and change, first made into language, then into idea, then into more tangible action." I stop; I don't quite understand. I roll her words *revelatory, distillation, predicate* around and around. I open my dictionary and thesaurus, dive into definitions and meanings, reaching toward something that feels entirely elusive. What do I need in order to embrace my justice dreams without reluctance? I springboard from Lorde's ideas and images: The light within which we *affirm* our dreams, *anchor* our dreams, *distill* our dreams down to their most elemental. Dreams cradled inside poetry, gardening, science, stargazing, seed collecting. Dreams affirmed, anchored, distilled. Dreams revealing the very essence of the worlds we need and long for.

I open my hands. Return to Aurora Levins Morales's invitation.

Black historian Robin D. G. Kelley writes in *Freedom Dreams* about the exact kind of claiming Morales is urging, "Call me utopian, but I inherited my mother's belief that a map to a new world is in the imagination, in what we see in our third eyes rather than in the desolation that surrounds us. Now that I look back . . . the kind of politics to which I've been drawn have more to do with imagining a different future than being pissed off about the present." Yes, and as a cranky activist, I want to be both a dreamer and righteously angry.

So many emotions accompany my justice dreaming. Sometimes my throat softens, and before joy or curiosity, I feel afraid. I fear the unknown, the immensity of my longing, the tenderness surging through my bodymind.

We gather, encourage each other, knowing that dreaming is often vulnerable work/play. We ask: *What would we do with our superpowers?* The answers vary widely:

> Ensure safe, stable homes for everyone.
> Sequester carbon.
> Transform greed.
> Vaporize shame and coercion.
> Replenish the aquifers.

Audre Lorde's words urge us toward the center, unfolding a progression where dreams weave into language, language bridges into idea, idea expands into action. And from there, Aurora Levins Morales points us to the horizon. She teaches us that utopian dreams—our biggest, boldest, most hopeful and extravagant imaginings—can lead us into futures and shape strategies in the present.

We sit together, unleashing ourselves:

We practice photosynthesis.
Melt fracking equipment back to iron ore.
Invent wheelchairs undaunted by rain and sand.
Sashay through the accordion universe of time and space.

. . . . .

Dreams beckon us. Reach into the past-present-future. Unfurl the flamboyant and improbable. Reveal the essence.

Slowly, slowly I am learning their sheer tensile strength.

Let Rebellion Be Our Song

we who live in a nation lulled
sing with swamps and aquifers

we who consume in unspeakable quantities
sing with tributaries

we who spew carbon   spread asphalt
sing with back eddies and muskrat dens

we blunted by greed
sing with fish   frogs   salamanders

sing and sing again

branch of river
root of tree
crack in dam

Bulldozer's Lament /// Stealing the Moon

FORMAT NOTE: *Two tall, narrow poems share a single page. Speaking to each other, they dance. Starting on opposite edges—one on the left, the other on the right—they slide into the center, almost touch. Then return to the edges, still speaking. And repeat.*

You of the soft hands, hard eyes,
you who drive me, insist
I gouge and rip my kin,
fill me with diesel
to satiate my hunger,
you who drill, pump,
burn tears pulled from
the bottom of the planet:

Have you ever tried
to snatch the moon
from the sky, fold her up
like an accordion,
slip her into your back
pocket to play later,
a long slow waltz?

Once upon a time
I lived in a seam of iron,
called earthworms cousin, and then
you descended upon us.

Your thievery
will never work—she is not
a chocolate bar shoplifted
from the corner store or a peach
plucked from the neighbor's tree.

Every night I dream: my garish skin
beginning to peel, flake by flake,
oxygen nibbling my bones, rain
and wind soothing me until
I melt back to earth.

Neither sweet nor illicit,
she will climb out
of your pocket and roll
far, far away.

Do not
fill me with sorrow again.

Her slow dance
does not belong to us.

Greed

prompted by Sweet Honey in the Rock's song "Greed"

grab greed
by its taproots

    river of dreams
    cold and clear

drag those long
white tubers
out of the aquifers,
rainforests,
our own human hearts

    river of sunlight
    undammed

burn
that slithering
heap of roots
down to spark
and ash

stock exchange shrivels

    river of stardust
    river of seeds

riot of morning glories
blooming up the elevator shafts.

Fairview Training Center Closes (2000)

HISTORICAL NOTE: *Between 1908 and 2000, the state-run Fairview Training Center in Salem, Oregon, locked up more than ten thousand people deemed intellectually and developmentally disabled. Many people lived at Fairview for most of their lives. They ate; slept; grew up; worked; fell in love; paced; were drugged and restrained, punished and abused; tried to run away; rebelled; survived; and died there.*

FORMAT NOTE: *Two voices interwoven. The first anchored to the left margin. The second leaping away, farther right and italicized, separate from the first but always in relationship.*

Doors slam shut
for the last time.

> *shadows cast*
> *on walls*
> *painted pink*
> *green   eggshell blue*
> *but dingy*

Grasses grow tall, seedheads nod,
arsonists and graffiti artists descend.

> *cement blocks*
> *and mortar*
> *festooned*
> *with rules   soaked*
> *in urine*

The bricks ooze
and crumble.

> *isolation*
> *cage and razor*
> *strap   nowhere*
> *to hide*

Inside the rubble we plant our tears,
tend their soft translucent leaves.

> *selves rupture*
> *from selves   vanish*
> *into the dark*
> *breathing spaces*
> *between mortar*
> *and block*

We build trellises, carve names,
remember the living and the dead.

A Great Flock of Stories (1977, 504 Sit-In)

HISTORICAL NOTE: *I wrote this poem for the exhibit* Patient No More, *which tells a history of the 1977 disability rights sit-in at the Department of Health, Education, and Welfare offices in San Francisco. The action lasted for approximately a month and led to the signing of Section 504 of the Rehabilitation Act. Predating the 1990 Americans with Disabilities Act by thirteen years, Section 504 significantly protected disabled people's civil rights. I anchored this poem in the exhibit's mural of protest and sit-in photos.*

Each photo: one
story, two; two stories,
three; three stories,
four, multiplied.

I read the pins
and slogans: *No more*
negotiating. Enough.
Sign 504 now.
Solidarity.

Their
words
rumble.

What lies beneath
these photos: whose voices,
languages, poems?

I read the placards
they carried: *Access*
to work. Can't
back down. You might
break your neck.
Remove the stairs
or we'll level them.

Let
their
words
sink in.

They slept rebellion, argued
rebellion, strategized rebellion,
laughed, cried, refused

to back down. They wrote:
The hunger strike
is in its 15th day! Keep
your campaign promises.
Suffered enough. Please
no more. Bastante.

We stutter,
stim,
sign,
drool
our rebellion,

trail fingers across
this history, its cracks
and bumps. How much
have we lost
and whitewashed?

Not one but two, not
two but three—we need
a great flock of stories.

They gave us:
Disabled In Action.
Human rights
for all. 504
victory.

Let
these photos
be signposts, neither

the beginning nor the end.

Praise

Let us praise
our canes   braces   catheters
our crutches   air filters   wheelchairs
our ventilators   prostheses   hearing aids.

Sing ourselves familiar.

you who did not survive
the denial of a kidney transplant

Our stories
strain   wisp   whirl
out of us,

stars dusting
our lungs
tongues
pillows.

you who did not survive
health insurance greed

Praise our medicine bottles and tinctures,
ice packs and insulin pumps,
spasms and unrelenting pain.

Sing ourselves gnarly.

you who did not survive
the psych ward

We cook,
laugh,
lie down
to sleep.

Praise
our withered legs
feverish skin
aching heads.

Sing ourselves essential.

you who did not survive
COVID-19 and dementia alone in a nursing home

Dream a history   a rebellion
a universe of love notes:

this too will be evidence,
feathers and bones.

you who did not survive
police custody

Praise
our broken hearts.

Sing ourselves cherished.

May Day (2020)

Yesterday on the phone, longing looped
through your words: *i cannot imagine a world*

without capitalism. My heart lurched. I wanted
to cajole, quote Karl Marx, curl into a hollowed-out

redwood stump. In this time
of epidemic, our doors closed, windows

open, as we ward off virus
and worry about death, let us

turn off the news—funerals doubling
every three days. We who sing

from balconies and play klezmer music
on front stoops. We who check in

every day over text, phone, Zoom, Skype,
Facebook, Facetime: *how are your lungs,*

can you make rent this month, did you lose your job today,
are you hungry right now, do you have enough

insulin, estrogen, prozac, klonopin, blood pressure meds?
We who drive across town to deliver saltines,

fresh kale, chicken soup, half bottles
of Tylenol, the last box of face masks

to ex-lovers and best friends. We who have always
shared everything we had. We who keep

each other alive. We who will be turned away
from emergency rooms and denied

ventilators. We who will never
go to the hospital. We who will die

and we who will live. Wall Street crashing,
cruise ships docked, World Bank

panicked, renters and Amazon workers
striking: It is time. It is time. It is time

to listen to our grief and soothe our jangled
nerves—we must not relinquish imagination.

Enough

1.

I sleep easily, slumber steady and unbroken, particularly in the decades since I gained access to a universe of dreams. Sleep loose and gauzy against my skin. But so many of the people I love struggle with slumber. Nightmares jerk them into panic. The latest news of military strikes and hurricanes revs anxiety. Pain knots joints. Children require care at 2 a.m. Trauma burrows deep into cells. Or my beloveds rest, but ever so lightly, attuned to every creak and murmur.

Personal and daily, but also systemic and global, the social and material conditions of sleeplessness gnaw at our hearts, nerves, adrenal glands. Sleep squeezed around second shifts, split shifts, or the three minimum-wage jobs needed to pay the rent. Sleep sheltered by cardboard in city parks and alleyways. Sleep shaped by prisons, psych wards, and tent encampments. Sleep disrupted by police barging in at midnight, guns drawn. In her manifesto *Rest Is Resistance*, Tricia Hersey declares, "Sleep deprivation is a public health issue."

We need to reshape slumber into release and refuge, a drifting down to stillness.

2.

I watch you slog through sleeplessness. Nights stretch out. Anxiety and pain thicken. Sometimes you tumble into sleep just before dawn but not for long. You wake unrested, unmoored, occasionally desperate—nothing unusual, no crisis, just this ordinary grind. Some days you turn brittle, a drought-worn blade of grass. I fear that you might break and blow away. I, the solid sleeper, yearn to share my slumber with you.

If everyone floated inside plentiful rest—experienced sleep as resistance and possibility, dream dust and love note, medicine and map, common as dirt—who might we become?

3.

I conjure a past-present-future: You and I wade in a gentle high tide, the surf a bed of stars. My chest rumbles. I scoop up a handful of foam—part salt, part sweet—basil, lemon, and cardamom all at once. My great-great-grandmothers walk toward us. They say, "Pay attention. At high tide there is always enough sleep, just share it."

I don't mean these words as a metaphor, nor foam as an abstraction. Certainly I'm spinning a fanciful story. But for a moment, allow the substance cupped in my hands—salty sweet bubbles—to be the material manifestation of my solid and reliable slumber. A substance we can transport from sleeping to waking and circulate among ourselves. I dream of sleep collectives; sleep co-ops; informal sleep networks of neighbors, friends, extended chosen family.

4.
Resting inside the rhythm of moon and ocean, you and I pause, hold still until my slumber surges—deep inside ephemeral currents, highest of tides. We arrive on its crest. Your sleep wanes, bodymind restless. We scoop up handfuls of foam. Pass them back and forth. Wash each other's faces with the bubbles. I trail more through your hair. It drifts over your collarbone, sternum, wrists. And then we're floating together, skin touching skin, in long slumber; neither time, space, nor history intrudes.

. . . . .

Let me pause to ask: How do we build a past-present-future where sleep is communal, akin to library books, public transportation, community meals? I conjure sleep libraries, sleep buses, sleep potlucks—slumber transformed into a collective resource. In this past-present-future, rest is the province of the moon and tides, the realm of earthworms, a gift as essential as air and water.

. . . . .

We wade repeatedly in the foam, roll onto our bellies, morph into sea mammals. You grow less exhausted by the night. I scoop sleep by the handful into a bucket. "Careful, careful," my great-great-grandmothers call. "Ask for consent and never take the last little bit of foam. Leave just enough to nourish an ocean of slumber."

5.
You and I whisper to each other late at night, "Enough warm, dry, safe beds. Enough homes. Enough food. Enough clean air and water. Enough respectful, affirming health care. Enough sleep. Enough love. May there be enough."
    Sustenance washes through us.

6.
We build vats from old cisterns no longer used to collect rainwater, reshaping the red cedar planks and rusty steel bands. Those of us who are solid sleepers carry our sleep foam into the waking world, filling the vats until they overflow. In this past-present-future, we're still imagining our way out of capital-

ism, establishing practices that don't mirror the not-so-distant past of selling and buying. Our success is uneven.

I love accompanying my not-well-rested friends to the barns, warehouses, and kitchens where these repurposed cisterns live. Together we arrive with mason jars and coffee mugs to scoop up handfuls of slumber.

We construct community sleep bins, akin to compost piles, in front yards, alleyways, and city parks. Foam collected and turned, decomposed to its essence, salty-sweet crystals. Rest instigates rest. We shut our eyes, nestle into blankets.

We invite each other to wade, roll, scoot, crawl in the surf, giddy and laughing ourselves to sleep. We lie loose-limbed, near but not touching, our breath slowing together, foam bubbling across skin.

The vats, compost piles, crystals, frothy surf all communal resources: *enough* smells part salt, part sweet—basil, lemon, and cardamom all at once.

V

Kin

Pond Speaks

FORMAT NOTE: *On the left, the pond narrates their day-to-day. Slightly to the right and italicized, the pond celebrates light.*

down at the muddy
bottom i nestle
between boulders,

cradle a quarter
moon, even

in dream
she makes me
murmur,

        starlight
        shadow light
        cloud light   never alone

i feed the fishes
and wake to fog's
twisting spires,

wrapped in sun
and morning chill

        tree light
        rain light
        wind light   dance and dance

i hold sky
in my arms,

only then
forget
my edges.

Bear

1.
black bear
takes his morning
bath, belly

touching streambed,
water
lifting fur,

i open throat
ribcage   soles
of feet to him

he rolls
side to side,
current rushing
through bulk,

rhythm
resisting gravity

he rises,
haunches
heaving, ambles
downstream
into sun.

2.
his amble
enters mine—
a single
moment—

i drop
to all fours

weight shifts,
shoulder
then hip,

shoulder
then hip,

paws push
into needles, spruce,
larch, claws
catch earth,

'til I slip
back into
my human
skin,

simply
crawling
on hands
and knees

because
ground
steadies me.

Lake Champlain at Flood Level

Because
into the teeming
basin of yourself,
you welcome snowmelt
and rainfall, invite
wind to rise, waves
to rock and slam. Because

you harbor countless
birds, fish, boats, both
floating and sunk, reflect
sun, cloud, sky without
asking why. Because

you swallow endless
sewage, phosphates,
mercury, sleep
with junker cars, broken
bottles, concrete pilings, never
a chance to lie fallow. Because

you connect river
to ocean, and because
right now you cannot
contain it all, I sing
with your heaving waters
and all they have unmoored.

A Murmuration of Dreams

FORMAT NOTE: *Lines float on the page, descend diagonally toward the right margin, pause, clustering, steady for a moment before cascading back toward the left. Words swirl, cascade again, a billowing flock. Through all this motion, the thread of images remains distinct.*

> Sometimes we trip into our past as we endure the present, but freedom is always now. — Aja Monet, foreword to Kelley, *Freedom Dreams*

we slip
    love notes
        to each other   folded
               into
               the accordion of time.

          they sleep
          beneath
          our skin:

          galaxies
        cascading
     into velvet dark,

          human light
          no longer
          flooding
          every crevice

              . . . . .

fireweed piercing   brick,
                   virginia creeper   curling round,

we dip
our brushes
into the milky way,

paint abandoned
prisons thick
with stars,

dreaming ourselves
backward

forward
into that velvet
dark waterfall

. . . . .

dreams flare,
love notes
creak   and groan
ghostly
as humpback
songs—

they wrap
around us:

lullabies   diatribes,

past

and future

howling

through

our bodies

Inside Grief Time

FORMAT NOTE: *On the right margin, interspersed through the poem, a litany—or a calling—of names shapes the grief.*

stamp   shake
shimmy   moan:

                    Coya   Diane   Amber   Laura   Becca   Karl

memory whirls

       white pine offering comfort

who will lie in the mud with me,
shoulder blades pressed into muck:

                    PJ   Neil   Fern   Susan   Matt   LL

your stories
smells
favorite songs
remain

I wrap his leather around me:

                    Carmen   Judith   Stacey   Mel   Linus

I too have come
close
to death

but not
close enough
to know:

       white pine urging me to stay steady

how
insubstantial
did you
become:

feather   whisper   tendril

or heavy:

boulder   bone   pull of gravity?

I wear their medallion against my breastbone:

        Carrie   Martina   Naomi   Laura   Chris

we buried her
in a cardboard coffin
on a ridge where
red tails and vultures circle

who will warm the stones with me,
fingers curled around heat:

        Tanis   Heather   Alexander   MaryFrances   Liz

white pine reminding me to draw nourishment from earth

what
did you learn
in your leaving:

clap
of thunder
flap
of wing?

We Wander the Castro Bewildered (1985)

HISTORICAL NOTE: *This poem takes place on October 21, 1985. But it starts seven years earlier in 1978 after Harvey Milk was elected as the first out gay member of the San Francisco Board of Supervisors. In November 1978, Dan White, who sat on the board with Milk, assassinated him and Mayor George Moscone. After serving five years for voluntary manslaughter, White committed suicide on October 21, 1985. In 1985, when the poem takes place, the AIDS epidemic was raging in San Francisco. For more about Harvey Milk, see Shilts,* Mayor of Castro Street.

FORMAT NOTE: *This poem fractures four times, lines lurching, breaking, then continuing on the next line.*

After Harvey died, we walked
down Market Street, a procession
of forty thousand candles, and after
his unremorseful killer received
the lightest of sentences, we burned
cop cars at City Hall, and now:
what now, AIDS reverberates
everywhere—
                        round after round
of hospice care, late nights
at the ER, and endless funerals,
holding ourselves tight-lipped
while preachers rave about sin,
try to erase our lives.
                        So tempting
to celebrate in the streets, as if
that killer's suicide might actually be
retribution.
                        Hearts halfway
convinced, we remove our shoes, twirl
onto pavement, shimmy
through Delores Park.
                        But we know,
we know, sky asking us to cry:
Harvey will still be dead.

Turning Toward Each Other

1980: The summer before my seventeenth birthday, I spent a weekend in Portland. A girl from the backwoods, I had no skills yet to navigate the cacophony of a city—even one as slow and small as Portland. Still I fell in love with the arts and crafts fair tucked underneath the Burnside Bridge. Amid concrete pilings, I encountered tie-dyed T-shirts and walnut-brown cutting boards. Several months earlier Mount St. Helens had erupted seventy miles to the north, volcanic ash filling the gutters; everything I touched felt gritty. I remember watching a power chair user sell his poetry zines and broadsides. I could see that he, like me, lived with cerebral palsy.

I had no disability politics or community, no analysis of ableism. I didn't even know that word. I believed all the bullying, staring, invasive touch, invisibility, and lack of access I faced was my fault. I hated the sound and cadence of my slurring voice. I tried hard to hide.

Yet at a distance, I stood watching this poet, leaning toward him, recognizing myself. I couldn't even bear to say hello. This encounter sparked my first disability poem.

. . . . .

Watching a Cerebral Palsied Writer at Saturday Market
(written in 1981)

Arthur, I am Elizabeth,
let us shake
spastic right hands,
we face the same ocean
inside our heads,
if you write and I run,
if I write and you sit
at Saturday Market,
we are courageous cripples.
I cringe beneath careful hugs,
careful as though I am
one of those glass ships
that were for sale
in the booth next to yours,
ships that would break in
your strong spastic hands.

I imagine what you see:
you listen to them quietly stare,
and then walk away whispering
or they ask you about
work, writing, CP,
your hands grab the air
while your tongue
struggles to grab the answer
caught in your skull.

But we do everything we do
as only we know how,
as we run and write and sit
at Saturday Market.

·····

In 1981, the words, metaphors, stories with which I name myself here and now didn't even exist as glimmers in my heart. Nor did my literal name—Eli. Instead, I lived with a name my parents chose; a name attached to the gender assigned to me at birth; a name that feels to me, as a trans person, utterly private and personal. But I've decided not to change a single word of my forty-year-old poem. Instead I want to crack open the shifting, unsteady work of naming ourselves and each other into existence.

Turning, turning, we need the rhythms of limp, spasm, seizure, quaking of aspen.

·····

2020: Out of the depths of my filing cabinets, I pull "Watching a Cerebral Palsied Writer at Saturday Market." It fills me with quiet tenderness: this bare-boned poem, a birch tree in the middle of winter. I can feel my younger self—that lonely disabled girl on the cusp of coming out as queer—her words leaning in to an imagined encounter that she wasn't ready to have in real life.

Remembering blurry fragments of that long-ago afternoon, I decide to rewrite the poem, turn again toward the image of delicate glass ships and strong spastic hands. To this process, I bring the disability communities that have saved my life over the last four decades, the home I've built with queer and trans disabled people.

Together we fine-tune the art of noncompliance and snarky answers. Learn the histories. Fashion the pry bars.

. . . . .

You at Saturday Market
(written in 2020, a rewriting of my 1981 poem "Watching a Cerebral Palsied
Writer at Saturday Market")

1.
We shake spastic
right hands, grin lopsided
at each other, your tremors
reaching into mine. I sit
on a creaky wooden chair
and we talk slow,
a rhythm of stop
and go, knee to knee,
hands flying. What
we say and what we don't:
songbirds and ghosts.

2.
You know, you know:
they pat my head,

kiss my cheek,
sometimes cry,

sometimes stink—perfume
and sweat—but always careful,

careful as if my bones
might break, delicate

as the glass schooners for sale
two booths down. I imagine

crystalline spires shattering
in your strong sexy hands.

You know every damn word
of their withering pity.

3.
They interrupt us with vacant
inquiries about your poetry
zines, zany broadsides, never
pausing for your replies
that arrive in bursts
of uneven words—first
daffodils of spring. They turn
to me, ask if you have this
diagnosis or that, surprised
by my slurred refusals.
Better when they leave, except
you need their five-dollar bills
for coffee and rent. I linger,
forget you're a stranger,
ignore the spitting rain.

. . . . .

Knee to knee, hip to hip, we gather the bare bones of midwinter, the lush
leaves of late summer, dreams so tender we can barely conjure them.

We, Two-Stepping Through Time

remember

before the first whaling ships leave port
and after the last oil wells run dry:

remember

we, picking the locks, flinging the doors open:

remember

we, renovating two-car garages into apothecaries,
goats in the front yard, chickens roaming free:

remember

before the existence of ownership,
after the abolishing of money:

remember

we, turning golf courses into vegetable gardens:

remember

we, tending the soil, ninth hole a tangle
of tomatoes and squash in late August:

remember

because forgetting
is as dangerous
as shame.

Great River Birds

Headed east
by train, we clank
over the Mississippi,
metal against metal,

ice still edging the banks,
birds swirl into air, scatter.
I lean against the cool slick

window, white settler
crossing Ioway, Dakota,
Meskwaki waters.

White wings tipped
with black: great river birds,
we have not met.

I holler
to the engineer,
stop, simply stop,

history squeals and sparks.

I clamber down
to ground, lay myself
in the reeds,

watch you land
again, nestle
into river,

a million stars
stashed in your long
orange bills, all bone
and gauzy sac,
feathers alight:

if I stay still
long enough,
might I join
the fishes, riffles,
gravel beneath
your bellies?

Sugar Maple

FORMAT NOTE: *Centered on the page, the lines unfold into the symmetrical shape of a bushy sugar maple—narrow at the top, spreading gradually to a wide middle, tapering to a narrow short trunk, and finally rooted in wide, flat ground.*

Not
long ago
I lived with a
sugar maple who
kept me company as
I wrote, a big oval-shaped
tree, bigger by the year, filling my
window, bare boned in winter and lush
green in summer, a steady presence, my words,
her breath, orange-gold luminescence and seeds
twirling to ground, finest of comrades: we were
never lovers, I regret to report, and then I left
the ridge, moved into town, my heart
still aches. But hers, pumping sap
as surely as blood, pulse
in tendril
of root and palest of green: her fine-grained heart,
hidden deep, loves earth, wind, sun, rain, worms in equal measure.

How to Love for the Long Haul

Remember:
love is a muscle
the size of our hearts,
open hands,
wild open sky.

Practice every day:
love fiddleheads, coyotes,
white pines, love red foxes
and barn cats, our own
round bellies, love the first ripe
cherry tomato, the last bite
of pesto, raucous call
of crows and deep quiet
of snow, love bone and gristle,
tendon and nerve, each other's
tender hearts.

Do not succumb
to ownership
or jealousy.

Love through long
rain, intense drought, love
in bookstores and kitchens,
alleyways and traffic jams,
at countless protests
and pride parades.

Love even when angry,
ashamed, heartbroken.

Become a sunflower
leaning into the sun.

White Pine

FORMAT NOTE: *Two voices interspersed: On the left, a love song to a single white pine. On the right, histories and ecologies of white pine forests.*

we climb branch over branch into your crown
small fists of cones opening

                        you of sweet pungent lemon pitch,
             confiscated by the British Royal Navy,
                      whittled down to ship masts.

we descend into your root ball
seeds flaring on wind

fists of prayers
fists of tears

                 you of multiple spires and cracked limbs:
                     a billion board feet milled
               year after year in the early 1900s.

we dream into your deep-throated hush
promises winging their way to earth

                     you, of furrowed skin,
               remain—snag, stump,
             rotten log covered in moss.

love song
dream song
trembling in the velvet dark song

wind plays a three-part harmony

honey-gold heart
beats   steady, steady.

Notes

A Cluster of Practices

xvi   *Sentient and nonsentient merge*   For more about objects, humanness, and personhood, see Kim, "Unbecoming Human."

xvi   *justice dreaming, is also collective and communal*   My use of *justice dreaming* spins off from historian Robin D. G. Kelley's phrase *freedom dreams*. See Kelley, *Freedom Dreams*.

Access Practices

xix   *We learn them from each other*   I have been taught access practices by dozens of people in cross-disability communities. Gratitude particularly to Robin Stephens and Corbett O'Toole. I've learned much from them as they have created access over the decades at cross-disability gatherings, large and small. For more about access practices, see Dolmage, *Academic Ableism*; Hamraie, *Building Access*.

xix   *accessible language also works in tandem with the disability access practices*   Many gratitudes to this lesbian-feminist tradition of accessible language. Of particular importance for me as a writer, reader, and student of accessible language is the work of Paula Gunn Allen, Dorothy Allison, Gloria Anzaldúa, Beth Brant, Chrystos, Judy Grahn, June Jordan, Melanie Kaye/Kantrowitz, Irena Klepfisz, Audre Lorde, Cherríe Moraga, Pat Parker, Minnie Bruce Pratt, Kate Rushin, and Nelle Wong. It's important to note that disability rarely shows up, at least explicitly, in their writings, either as named identity, content, or access practice.

Accessible language is also part of Language Justice. For a concise explanation of how Language Justice and Disability Justice are connected, see Sins Invalid, "Language Justice Is Disability Justice." For important thinking about speech, communication, language, and disability access, see Baggs, "Up in the Clouds and Down in the Valley"; Sequenzia and Grace, *Typed Words, Loud Hands.*

xix   *an insistence on sensory bodymind-based experience*   The word *bodymind* resists the white Western categorization of body as separate from mind. This classification scheme prioritizes minds and establishes them as a defining characteristic of personhood. *Bodymind* declares that our bodies always include our minds and our minds in turn shape our embodied experiences in thousands of ways. I use *bodymind* and *body* somewhat idiosyncratically throughout the book. I often choose the former when the entangled nature of body and mind is particularly apparent or pertinent. For more, see Price, "Bodymind Problem and the Possibilities of Pain"; Raffo, *Liberated to the Bone.*

xx   *that word itself, a tool of ableist-sexist-antipoor white supremacy*   For more about how the word *stupid* is used as a weapon against poor and working-class people, particularly in higher education, see Kadi, "Stupidity 'Deconstructed.'"

xx   *an access practice I've not encountered before*   Gratitude to everyone who helped me think about the access practice of format notes and shape the notes themselves into useful tools: Catherine Kudlick, Elizabeth Ault, Georgina Kleege, Ian Sutherland, Kevin Gotkin, and Susan Burch. All the mistakes and the ways in which the notes may not live up to their intent are fully my responsibility.

xxi   *citations as a community-based practice of interdependence, gratitude, and access*   Many gratitudes to the framework of Disability Justice for centering the importance of interdependence. For more on this subject, see Kafai, *Crip Kinship*; Levins Morales, *Kindling*; Nishida, *Just Care*; Piepzna-Samarasinha, *Care Work*; Erickson, "Thinking About and with Collective Care."

xxi   *these standards have, more recently*   For more details, see Autistic Self Advocacy Network, "One Idea per Line"; Acton, "Plain Language for Disability Culture."

xxii   *using plain language standards to shape my words*   For important reflections on and critiques of accessible language and plain language, see Chen, "Chronic Illness, Slowness, and the Time of Writing." In the current world, where English is a dominant language and a tool/weapon of past and present colonization and coerced assimilation, how we practice accessible language/communication needs to take multiple forms, shaped by readers' and writers' languages (signed, spoken, and/or written), cultures, communities, education, class, and disability.

At the same time, Alice Wong provides a powerful model for leaning in to plain language. After she edited the anthology *Disability Visibility*, she commissioned Sara Luterman to translate the book into plain language, making it available as a free download (Luterman, "Plain Language Translation of *Disability Visibility*").

xxii   *an act of collective care*   At its most basic, *collective care* refers to mutual care given and received within community, often intentionally outside the institutional structures of the medical-industrial complex, charity, and state-funded social safety nets. Both the framework and practices of *collective care* are being developed and nuanced within the context of Disability Justice in tandem with practices of interdependence. Gratitude to Loree Erickson for many kitchen table conversations about her care collective.

xxii   *useful and incomplete*   Gratitude to the feminist antiviolence activists who have developed powerful trigger-warning practices over the decades. For more about content notes/trigger warnings and disability access, see Kafer, "Un/Safe Disclosures"; Carter, "Teaching with Trauma."

xxiii   *I paused again and again*   For a deep dive into self-care framed by both politics and lived experience, see Ortiz, *Sustaining Spirit*; Kim and Schalk, "Reclaiming the Radical Politics of Self-Care."

Prelude

Kisses, Fists, and Underground Rivers

3   *I decided to take a chance*   Gratitude to Bill Beckman, who taught English, journalism, and poetry at Pacific High School, for nourishing me and making his classroom a lunchtime refuge; to Barbara Drake, the first poet I knew personally who wrote books and published poems; and to

my poetry classmates for every single mediocre and enthusiastic poem we wrote and shared with each other.

4   *underground rivers*   Gratitude to Leah Lakshmi Piepzna-Samarasinha and their poem "dirty river girl," where underground rivers are both very literal and powerfully metaphoric (Piepzna-Samarasinha, *Bodymap*, 29–34).

4   *Didn't feel bold*   Gratitude to Wild Wimmin for Peace, an ensemble group on the Great Peace March—eighteen of us writing songs, changing lyrics, reciting poetry, making art out of feminist rage and grief. I can still feel the tingle of adrenaline as I held a mic close, reciting my poem about the Seneca Army Depot. As soon as I finished, Trish Flynn's voice would rise in the dark, singing Judy Small's antiwar song "Bridget Evans."

Heart

6   *Heart*   Gratitude to Stacey Park Milbern (1997–2020) and PJ Redbird Two Ravens (1965–2022). I began writing this poem during the early COVID-19 pandemic before and after Stacey's death. I finished the poem for PJ's memorial service.

A Korean queer Disability Justice activist, Stacey wrote, organized, and loved disabled people, particularly disabled Black, Indigenous, and other people of color (BIPOC). Stacey and I followed each other's work from afar and saw each other whenever and wherever we could. For a sampling of Stacey's work, see Piepzna-Samarasinha and Wong, "#StaceyTaughtUs Syllabus."

A gender and sex outlaw, social worker, and queer/trans organizer, PJ held space for hundreds, if not thousands, of trans people to come out in Michigan in the 1990s and early 2000s. He facilitated the trans/gender-nonconforming support group Gender Explorers that I attended in the late 1990s. That space made my trans coming out more possible. I could not have written these words without Stacey's and PJ's presence in my heart. I send both of them big love.

Unfurl: An Invitation

7   *Unfurl: An Invitation*   This poem (and really this whole book) started with an invitation from Alice Sheppard of the disability arts ensemble Kinetic Light. She, Laurel Lawson,

and Michael Maag (along with an unforgiving and revelatory ramp/stage set) were in the midst of creating DESCENT, a disabled, queer, multiracial love story told in dance. Alice asked me to write a poem for the performance to be used as part of sonic access for blind, low vision, and nonvisual audience members. Out of her request emerged "Unfurl: An Invitation." Bodyminds in motion — unfolding to music, light, rhythm — totally shaped my words, and in turn my stanzas sometimes informed Kinetic Light's choreography. Unfurling was never solely conceptual or metaphorical in our collaboration but actual, held in muscle, emotion, and story. Many gratitudes for this collaboration. Alice, thank you for inviting me into this disability art and access making.

11   *become the gliding / of her wheels*   Gratitude to power chair–using poet, Green Party member and one-time political candidate, journalist, and ADAPT activist Martina Robinson. I learned about the joy of this particular kind of invitation to dance from her. At one of the Society for Disability Studies dances, she invited me onto her lap and swooped us around the perimeter of the dance floor.

I. Tremors

Your Tremoring Hands and Mine

19   *of politeness*   Gratitude to the many queer/trans disabled people who have taught me how to unlearn compliance and embrace fierce gimpy noncompliance. MaryFrances Platt and Sebastian Margaret have repeatedly revealed the power of snarky humor to me.

Remember

20   *a dailiness of tremors*   Gratitude to all the beings that tremor — ranging from the planet to quaking aspen to the human bodyminds who reflect, hold, love my shakiness. Without all of you, I could never have reimagined tremoring from a shameful experience to a common one.

20   *dolomite scraping / over shale*   Gratitude to the thrust fault along Lake Champlain, unceded ancestral Abenaki territory, for the strong yellow-gold rock overlaying flaky gray-black stone and for the eons of tremors.

Never Still: Eclipse over Ricker Pond

22   *Never Still: Eclipse over Ricker Pond*   Gratitude to the full moon rising over unceded ancestral Abenaki territory.

River

24   *river of stutter*   Gratitude to JJJJJerome Ellis for making connections between stuttering and tremoring (Ellis, *Clearing*, 42–43).

Moving Close to the Ground: A Messy Love Song

27   *Moving Close to the Ground: A Messy Love Song*   Gratitude to Alice Sheppard. Her solo dancing outside among trees in a variety of wheeled and crutched embodiments, sometimes moving very close to the ground, opens more space for my own crawling and scooting embodiments. Gratitude to Alison Kafer for many outdoor rolls and walks and much joy and connection along rivers and among trees. Gratitude to Julia Watts Belser for conversations about hiking while physically disabled, including the juicy details of our moves.

27   *sliding, scooting, crawling, crab walking*   I'm writing from a distinctly US, Global North context. In her article "'People of the Apokalis': Spatial Disability and the Bhopal Disaster," feminist disability studies scholar Jina Kim writes about the novel *Animal's People* and its main character, Animal, who is disabled by a multinational corporate-caused environmental disaster akin to the 1984 destruction caused by Union Carbide in Bhopal, India. Animal is a quadruped. Kim quotes him after he refuses a surgery that would allow him to walk: "I reckon that if I have this operation, I will be upright, true, but to walk I will need the help of sticks. I might have a wheelchair, but how far will that get me in the gullis of Khaufpur? Right now I can run and hop and carry kids on my back, I can climb hard trees, I've gone up mountains, roamed in jungles. Is life so bad?" Kim comments, "By underscoring Animal's mobility in the city of Khaufpur, this passage demonstrates how spatiality produces certain forms of embodiment. In the uneven and gutted topography of Khaufpur, where curb cuts and other paths of access do not even register as concerns, a wheelchair would greatly compromise movement, as it is designed for flat, even, and paved terrain. In the context of Khaufpur, Animal is not disabled, but especially abled. Ability emerges as a socio-spatial

experience, and because he can easily access and navigate Khaufpur's terrain, his body is no longer legible as disabled." Thank you to Alison Kafer for bringing Kim's article to my attention.

The particular disability community silence I'm writing about is shaped by relatively easy access to wheeled mobility, by a relative abundance of access features like ramps and curb cuts, and by "flat, even, and paved terrain." In other words, this silence isn't about crawling in and of itself but crawling and not crawling in a well-resourced (relatively and unevenly) Global North nation-state.

27   *mostly in isolation*   The pleasures of moving close to the ground are abundant in the more-than-human world that isn't paved with asphalt or covered with concrete. In places more frequented by humans, what we throw away and excrete, along with fossil-fuel-guzzling machines, often makes the ground unpleasant and sometimes disgusting, stinky, and/or dangerous, particularly by Global North standards.

27   *As an unsteady walkie*   *Walkie* is a disability community word to describe people who walk rather than roll. It isn't intended to create a walking/rolling binary. Disabled people know there are thousands of ways to walk and thousands of ways to roll, and many of us do both. Rather, *walkie* makes visible a privileged mode of mobility that is taken entirely for granted in the nondisabled world.

27   *Neither a protest against ableism*   A relatively simple, blunt, and straightforward definition of *ableism*: a system of discrimination/oppression targeting disabled and chronically ill people and those perceived as such. It manifests as violence; lack of access to employment, housing, transportation, education, decent health care, and more; isolation; institutionalization; invisibility and hypervisibility; a devaluing of our lives (better dead than disabled); and a whole host of stereotypes. This straightforward definition tells part of the story but doesn't push far enough. Black disabled abolitionist, artist, educator, and community lawyer Talila A. Lewis writes that ableism is "a system of assigning value to people's bodies and minds based on societally constructed ideas of normalcy, productivity, desirability, intelligence, excellence, and fitness. These constructed ideas are deeply rooted in eugenics, anti-Blackness, misogyny, colonialism, imperialism, and capitalism. This systemic oppres-

sion leads to people and society determining people's value based on their culture, age, language, appearance, religion, birth or living place, 'health/wellness,' and/or their ability to satisfactorily re/produce, 'excel' and 'behave.' You do not have to be disabled to experience ableism" (Lewis, "Working Definition of Ableism"). These two definitions side by side name a lot of what ableism is and does, but of course there is more—much activism, whole books, and many library shelves devoted to the contexts, nuances, histories, and present-day realities of ableism.

28   *offers me a hand*   Gratitude to my partner, Samuel Lurie, for the many ways we create access between us. In working over the years to take his hand without hesitation, I've learned so much about interdependence.

28   *not* clumsy *but* slow *and* intimate   For more on access intimacy, including a foundational definition, see Mingus, "Access Intimacy."

30   *neither saturated with nor defined by ableism*   For more about disability, ableism, and the more-than-human world, see Ray and Sibara, *Disability Studies and the Environmental Humanities*; Ortiz, *Rituals for Climate Change*; Taylor, *Disabled Ecologies*.

31   *I crawl wherever I can*   Brashear, *Fixed*. In contrast to Wolbring, transhumanist engineer Hugh Herr declares later in *Fixed*, "I mountain climb. I trail run. I play tennis. I do everything I want to do. If you remove the technology from my body, all I can do is crawl. I'm completely crippled." His blunt words reflect an intense connection between attitudes toward crawling and the devaluing of disability.

31   *as rebellious and matter-of-fact as Wolbring*   In her review of *Fixed*, feminist disability studies theorist Alison Kafer uses the contrast between Wolbring and Herr (mentioned in the previous note) to think about the tension that surrounds crawling. She writes: "I admit to a thrill of recognition here. Herr's comments explain why we so rarely see images of disabled people crawling—other than for purposes of protest or performance—but . . . *here's hoping Wolbring's appearance sparks more documentation of this everyday (yet spectacularly stigmatized) modality*" (Kafer, "Fixed"; emphasis added). Her call sparked me to write specifically and frankly about my experiences of moving close to the ground.

32   *the newly renovated and disability-accessible Galehead Hut*   For more about this trek, see Northeast Passage, "Trek to Galehead."

32   *Let's eat that rock*   Goldberg, "For These Trailblazers, Wheelchairs Matter."

II. Survivals and Sorrows

Ruptures

35   *Ruptures*   Big gratitude to Susan Burch, Joe Kadi, Samuel Lurie, Sebastian Margaret, Aurora Levins Morales, and Susan Raffo for making space for these stories, thinking with me, collaborating on genealogical research that I could never have done by myself, and helping me stay anchored to the present. Here's to community, access, and interdependence.

36   *Ceded in 1872–73*   For more on the Homestead Act, white homesteading, and its impact on Indigenous peoples, see National Archives, "Homestead Act (1862)"; Wilm, "'Indians Must Yield'"; White, *"It's Your Misfortune and None of My Own"*; Veracini, "Settler Colonialism Is Not Finished."

36   *ceded in 1863*   For more about the 1863 treaty, see Benoit and Marshall, *Treaty at Old Crossing*; Red Lake Nation, "Tribal History & Historical Photos."

37   *a system intent on the erasure*   For another account about a white settler family's legacy of farming on stolen Lakota homeland, see Clarren, *Cost of Free Land*. In her blend of investigative journalism and memoir, Rebecca Clarren returns several times to the question of what her ancestors knew and understood about the Lakota homeland they occupied. From my viewpoint in relationship to my white settler ancestors, the answers to this question are inconsequential. Whatever they knew or didn't, deflected or denied, they caused great harm and operated from deep ruptures.

37   *The US Army massacred hundreds of Lakota people at Wounded Knee*   For more about the massacre at Wounded Knee, see Treuer, *Heartbeat of Wounded Knee*; Gonzalez and Cook-Lynn, *Politics of Hallowed Ground*; Ostler, *Plains Sioux and U.S. Colonialism*.

37   *A thundering absence*   For more about the century-long bison massacre in the United States, see Jawort, "Genocide by
Other Means"; Hixson, *American Settler Colonialism*; Graybill, "Rangers, Mounties, and the Subjugation of Indigenous
Peoples."

37   *Removed thousands of children*   For more about Canton
Asylum for Insane Indians, see Yellow Bird, "Wild Indians";
Whitt, "'Care and Maintenance'"; Gregory, "Competency,
Allotment, and the Canton Asylum"; Burch, *Commit-
ted*. For more about boarding schools, see Child, *Boarding
School Seasons*; Lomawaima et al., "Editors' Introduction to
the Special Issue"; Woolford, *This Benevolent Experiment*;
Trafzer et al., *Boarding School Blues*; Adams, *Education for
Extinction*.

37   *Indigenous personhood, survivance, and kin*   For foundational work on survivance, see Vizenor, *Manifest Manners*;
Vizenor, *Survivance*.

Hallucinations

41   *knee-deep / mud*   Gratitude to all the beings—more-than-
human and human—who helped me survive that summer. I
particularly want to name Billie—stubborn and cuddle dog
supreme—baby beets and baby potatoes, the maple and crab
apple trees, and my spirit grandmothers.

Lean Close

44   *a fiddle fine grained / and singing*   Every time I sit with my
friend Deirdre Kelly and listen to fiddle music, I think about
spruce trees and all the sounds they make in the forest.

44   *Superfund site*   For important thinking and histories about
land and the refusal to abandon place-based connection
amid environmental destruction/devastation, see Taylor,
Disabled Ecologies; Voyles, *Wastelanding*.

The Trapdoor of Time

49   *not sorrow time*   Writing about different kinds of time, particularly in relationship to my father's death, has led me back
to work and conversations about crip time. Gratitude to all
the ways, both in their work and in our friendships, that Ellen Samuels, Alison Kafer, Mel Chen, and Margaret Price
have opened up the bendy, loopy nature of time in relationship to madness, chronic illness, and disability. See Kafer,
Feminist, Queer, Crip; Kafer, "After Crip, Crip After"; Sam-

uels and Freeman, "Introduction"; Samuels, "Six Ways of Looking at Crip Time"; Chen et al., *Crip Genealogies*; Price, *Crip Spacetime*; Price, "Bodymind Problem."

49   *cedar comfort me*   Every morning for months after my father's death, I walked along Lake Champlain in Oakledge Park, unceded ancestral Abenaki territory. I talked to the trees, swung on the swings, and cried my heart out. I found so much solace there. Thank you.

50   *a smart and funny friend*   I first found my father's obituary through Google. This weird circumstance is one of the many ways long-term estrangement plays out. And then I located his obit again on Facebook along with dozens of comments. Days after my successful Google search, blurry with grief-rage-numbness at 1 a.m., I posted a private request on my Facebook page for stories about deaths of perpetrators and estranged family members. The outpouring of responses, stories, and care supported me through that time.

51   *swallow the lies of the settler colonial nation-state*   Calling the United States a settler colonial nation-state names a fundamental truth about this country and settler colonialism as a force of domination. A beginning definition from the "Settler Colonial Primer":

> In settler colonialism land . . . is key. . . . Indigenous Peoples are literally replaced by settlers. Indigenous Peoples are erased through outright genocide, assimilation and interbreeding (including rape). . . . Settlers are . . . different from other colonizers in that they are there to stay, unlike in other colonial systems where the colonizer returns to their home country after profiting. Here, the land itself is the profit. Another important concept in understanding this system is the idea that in settler colonialism, "invasion is a structure not an event." This means that settler colonialism is not just a vicious thing of the past, such as the gold rush, but exists as long as settlers are living on appropriated land and thus exists today. (Hurwitz and Bourque, "Settler Colonial Primer")

Many gratitudes to Coya White Hat-Artichoker (Lakota) and the First Nations Two Spirit Collective for their deep political education work about Indigenous sovereignty and history. I've learned much from their work in non-Indigenous queer and trans social justice organizing spaces.

For nuanced history and analysis of settler colonialism, see Dunbar-Ortiz, *Not "A Nation of Immigrants"*; Wolfe, "Settler Colonialism and the Elimination of the Native"; Kauanui, "'A Structure, Not an Event'"; Hernández, *City of Inmates*. For the interlocking of settler colonialism and patriarchy, see Deer, *The Beginning and End of Rape*.

Fifty Years After He Beat Me

53   *Fifty Years After He Beat Me*   Gratitude to craniosacral bodyworker Rex Dazzle of Yarrow Integrative Healing for holding me and the process of releasing trauma and fear with skill and heart. I started this poem on their table, words forming as their hands and wisdom supported my body-mind in this release.

The Art of Disassociation

54   *escape artists / efficient and beautiful*   Gratitude to Mad activists, Mad politics, Mad studies, and most of all Mad pride for creating brilliant resistance, counteracting shame, and carving space out to claim our messiest selves in our most extreme and most mundane states. See landry et al., "Toronto: How Do We Win?"; Gorman, "Mad Nation?"; Curtis et al., *Mad Pride*; LeFrançois et al., *Mad Matters*; Kunzel, "Queer History, Mad History, and the Politics of Health."

pause   pause

55   *Sister Rosetta rising / in feet hips shoulders*   For more about Sister Rosetta Tharpe, the often overlooked Black queer godmother of rock and roll, see Wald, *Shout, Sister, Shout!*

A Murmuration of Survival

57   act up / fight back fight AIDS   For histories of the AIDS/ HIV epidemic and activism, see Schulman, *Let the Record Show*; Watkis-Hayes, *Remaking a Life*; Strub, *Body Counts*; Schneider and Stoller, *Women Resisting AIDS*; Schalk, "More Than Just Prevention"; France, *How to Survive a Plague*.

Gratitude to Rebecca Denison for all the conversations about HIV+ women and AIDS/HIV activism and all her work at WORLD (Women Organized to Respond to Life-Threatening Diseases).

58   *JUST / DROP MY BODY / ON THE STEPS / OF THE F.D.A.*
      For details about David Wojnarowicz and a photo of his
      famous activist denim jacket, see Carr, *Fire in the Belly*,
      400.

59   *on the steps / of the* NRA   Gratitude to youth anti–gun vio-
      lence activists, who have borrowed David Wojnarowicz's
      AIDS activist slogan and remixed it. See, for example, Ryan,
      "Best Signs from Iowa's National School Walkout Rally."

III. Moving Toward Porousness

Creating Categories

65   Cerebral palsied, Women, *and* United States   Thank you
      to Amelia Bowen Koford, whose interview with me in 2011
      encouraged me to think critically about these subject head-
      ings. See Koford, "Engaging an Author."

65   cerebral palsied   For more about the functions of diagnosis
      from a disability activist lens, see Clare, *Brilliant Imperfec-
      tion*; Kim, *Curative Violence.*

66   *don't match medicalized definitions of female and male*   Tell-
      ingly, there are no diagnostic categories that explain, pathol-
      ogize, and shame the sexed and gendered bodyminds of
      white, blue-eyed, masculine (as defined by US white middle-
      class nondisabled expectations) males easily read as hetero-
      sexual cisgender men. Fundamentally, diagnosis is used only
      to name and police conditions and bodyminds deemed ab-
      normal or deviant.

67   *from enslaved Black people*   For more about the United
      States as a nation-state built on the coerced labor of en-
      slaved Black people and stolen land of Indigenous peoples,
      see Dunbar-Ortiz, *Not "A Nation of Immigrants"*; Dunbar-
      Ortiz, *Indigenous Peoples' History of the United States*; Mays,
      Afro-Indigenous History of the United States; Jones, "Labor
      and the Idea of Race in the American South."

67   *it does not exist*   Madeline Veitch, email to author, August
      1, 2013.

67   *from* Handicapped *to* People with disabilities   For a history
      of how disability-related subject headings have shifted over
      time, see Sullivan, "Contextualizing Disability."

68   *genderqueer people*   Madeline Veitch, email to author, August 1, 2013.

68   *decenter settler colonial nation-states*   See, for example, the X̱wi7x̱wa (pronounced whei-wha) Library, a branch of the University of British Columbia library system. The more than five thousand Indigenous-centered volumes shelved in this branch are categorized using a classification system created by Kahnawá:ke librarian Brian Deer. He developed this system in the 1970s for the National Indian Brotherhood. From there, he cataloged the library at the Union of British Columbia Indian Chiefs. In both places, he created a system to match a specific set of books rather than a classification scheme that could be used more widely or universally. His brother Philip Deering talks about Deer's work as "an example of traditional Haudenosaunee's culture of adaptation." He says, "We have the Ohén:ton Karihwaté́hkwen the idea of which, you would never say it the same way twice even the same speaker. . . Brian was following that oral tradition by cataloguing differently every time that he catalogued a collection. It was adapted to each collection" (quoted in Rowe, "Humble Intellectual Leaves Unique Legacy"; ellipses in original). Deer's systems embed Native worldviews into how books are arranged on the shelves, grouping them by Indigenous nation and tribe and then grouping nations and tribes together by geography to emphasize kinship connections to one another and to the land. He also crafted subject headings that reflect the primary concerns and interests of First Nations and uses the names Native peoples choose for themselves. For more about Deer's life, see Weihs, "Tribute to Brian Deer."

The X̱wi7x̱wa Library has modified Deer's work to fit its specific collection. The website explains that "X̱wi7x̱wa means 'echo' in Sḵwx̱wú7mesh Sníchim (Squamish language). . . . The mandate of the X̱wi7x̱wa Library is to 'echo' the voices and philosophies of Indigenous people through its services, collections, and programs" (University of British Columbia, "About X̱wi7x̱wa Library").

68   *work to regain it*   Madeline Veitch, email to author, January 3, 2023.

68   *how slow and grinding change often is*   I've learned these lessons over the decades from activist elders Suzanne Pharr, Amber Hollibaugh, Miss Major, Aurora Levins Morales, and

Corbett O'Toole. They teach me through their writings, books, speeches, trainings, organizing, kindness, tenacity, and long-haul dreams. Many, many gratitudes. For a sampling of their work, see Pharr, *Transformation*; Hollibaugh, *My Dangerous Desires*; Meronek and Griffin-Gracy, *Miss Major Speaks*; Levins Morales, *The Story of What Is Broken Is Whole*; O'Toole, *Fading Scars*.

Turning Away from Categories

71   *right here, right now*   Gratitudes to Curtis Walker for his clarity, kindness, and disability politics as we sat together that afternoon. Through that experience, my entire body-mind absorbed important lessons about access, disabled queer/trans connection, and collective care.

Your Breath in the Pixels

72   *Your Breath in the Pixels*   Gratitude to Cal Montgomery, good friend of Mel Baggs and fierce disability activist and writer, for his time, attention, and brilliance. Under arduous conditions, he generously read an early draft of this poem. My words found their shape through his feedback, which, among other things, helped me focus how I wanted to remember Mel and hir work.

72   where I belong in the world   Baggs, "About."

72   that shut me out   Baggs, "Empty Mirrors and Redwoods."

74   *never traded rhythms*   References are to Baggs, "In My Language."

76   ground at all   Baggs, "Up in the Clouds and Down in the Valley."

76   when I grow up   Baggs, "Empty Mirrors and Redwoods."

When Categories Fail

77   *already exist*   The idea that we need to be dreaming liberatory futures while also working in the present to live inside them is deeply embedded in abolition and transformative justice politics. For instance, see Ben-Moshe et al., *Disability Incarcerated*; Ben-Moshe, *Decarcerating Disability*; Dixon and Piepzna-Samarasinha, *Beyond Survival*. I'm learning so much about dreaming freedom/living freedom from the work of Alexis Pauline Gumbs and adrienne maree brown.

Unclassifiable

78   *heat-rising-off-the-sidewalk*   Gratitude to trans and nonbinary communities where this explosion of unclassifiable genders is happening every day. Particular thanks to the femme brilliance of Holly Ferrise and Loree Erickson, with whom I have had these conversations for several decades.

IV. Dreams and Rebellions

Learning to Dream

84   *rhythm of my sleep*   Gratitudes beyond gratitudes to Joe Kadi for accompanying me through more than three decades of this work. For powerful short stories about this long-haul process, see Kadi, *Great Loss of the Twentieth Century*.

85   *tapering to a trickle*   My thinking about environmental damage and aquifers is tremendously shaped by Sunaura Taylor's work (Taylor, *Disabled Ecologies*).

86   *maintain the status quo*   Levins Morales, "Cripping the Great Turning."

86   *disabled ingenuity*   For other specific accounts of communal nourishings of liberatory imagination, see brown, "Outro," 280–81; Lewis, "birth of resistance." For more specifically about disability and liberatory futures, see Piepzna-Samarasinha, *The Future Is Disabled*.

87   *tangible action*   Lorde, *Sister Outsider*, 37.

87   *about the present*   Kelley, *Freedom Dreams*, 2–3.

88   *tensile strength*   Big gratitudes to Tourmaline, Syrus Marcus Ware, Aurora Levins Morales, and Amber Hollibaugh, all of whom have urged me into the necessity of dreaming.

Greed

91   *prompted by Sweet Honey in the Rock's song "Greed"*   Every time I think or write about greed, Dr. Bernice Johnson Reagon's big alto voice singing the song "Greed" echoes in my head and heart. Dr. Reagon (1942–2024)—renowned Black activist, cultural historian of music history, and founder of the Black women's acapella group Sweet Honey in the Rock—wrote "Greed" in the early 1990s. About its

origin, she told Amy Goodman in a 2003 *Democracy Now!* interview,

> I was thinking about human beings' capacity for evil and wondering if some of the things I saw human beings doing to each other was some place within me.... What is this thing that seems to sometimes make human beings get so lopsided in relationship to each other and in relationship to the world that supports them? And I kept coming up with greed, that somehow there is something about needing more than you need, not only wanting more than you need, where if you don't have more than you need, you're a failure.... [T]here's something very, very wrong with that. And there's a lot of destruction behind it. And so first I wrote "Greed" as a prose poem, and then I wondered if I could sing it. (Sweet Honey in the Rock, "Legendary Civil Rights Singers, Sweet Honey in the Rock")

I put this song on repeat as I wrote my poem "Greed." Gratitude beyond gratitude to Dr. Bernice Johnson Reagon for all her music, teachings, social justice work, and leadership.

Fairview Training Center Closes (2000)

92 *the last time* This poem started with Danielle Denham Skinner's photographs of Fairview's abandoned buildings after the institution's closure. See James, "Fairview Training Center May Have the Darkest History in Oregon." For a history of Fairview, see Ferguson et al., *"Away from the Public Gaze."* For stories told by former residents of living at Fairview, see Oregon Council on Developmental Disabilities, "Voices from Fairview."

A Great Flock of Stories (1977, 504 Sit-In)

94 mural of protest and sit-in photos For the mural and black-and-white protest photos I'm writing about and the exhibit about the 504 sit-in, see San Francisco State University, "Patient No More." For the individual photos, see San Francisco State University, "Section 504 Protest Mural." For a photo of the mural itself, see Stange, "'Patient No More' Show in Berkeley." (Visual description: A series of large black-and-white protest photos curve along a wall above a

portion of an indoor wheelchair ramp.) For more history of the disability rights movement, including the 504 sit-in, see Pelka, *What We Have Done.*

Praise

97   *Praise*   I wrote this poem to honor LL Gimeno, Carrie Ann Lucas, Laura Rauscher, Alexander Bear Goodrum, Judith McConnell, Tanisha Anderson, Sandra Bland, and so many more.

98   *this too will be evidence*   This line borrows from the title of Mia Mingus's blog *Leaving Evidence* (https://leaving evidence.wordpress.com).

98   *Sing ourselves cherished*   I wrote this line thinking of a photograph of Stacey Park Milbern. She sits in her wheelchair wearing a white tank top and dark-framed glasses. She smiles, head cocked to the side, her trach and vent tube visible. She holds a piece of paper in front of her with the word *cherished* written on it in black letters. For this photo, see Piepzna-Samarasinha and Wong, "#StaceyTaughtUs Syllabus."

In 2019 Stacey with the Disability Justice Culture Club and Max Airborne with Fat Rose were developing the #NoBodyIsDisposable campaign and organizing a Close the Camps demo in San Francisco (to protest the widespread detention of immigrants, including many children separated from their families, in inhumane, concentration camp–like conditions at the US border). As part of this work, they asked disability communities, fat communities, and queer/trans communities for words that are the opposite of *disposable.* The list was long: *kin, irreplaceable, worthy, valuable, wanted, treasured, sacred,* and *necessary,* among others. Stacey and Max also collected photos of people holding up signs printed with these words. Among these photos is the one of Stacey and the word *cherished.*

Enough

101   *in city parks and alleyways*   2024: I am finishing this piece days after the US Supreme Court declared constitutional the laws that ban houseless people from sleeping in public spaces. In her dissent, Justice Sonia Sotomayor wrote, "Sleep is a biological necessity, not a crime." See City of Grants Pass v. Johnson, 603 U.S. (2024) (Sotomayor, S., dissent-

ing). This ruling makes the material conditions of sleep even more intense and brutal for houseless people.

101   *a public health issue*   Hersey, *Rest Is Resistance*, 18.

101   *just share it*   In writing this imagining, I'm working within a long tradition of speculative fiction/science fiction as a location for justice dreaming. In *Octavia's Brood*, Walidah Imarisha and adrienne maree brown use the phrase *visionary fiction*. See Imarisha, "Introduction"; Schalk, *Bodyminds Reimagined*.

102   *an ocean of slumber*   As I imagine asking the ocean and tide for consent before gathering sleep foam, I follow the lead of Robin Wall Kimmerer (Potawatami), who writes about asking plants for permission and listening carefully for their answers before gathering them. See Kimmerer, *Braiding Sweetgrass*.

V. Kin

Pond Speaks

107   *my edges*   Many gratitudes to Ricker Pond in unceded ancestral Abenaki territory for all the teachings and connections, and their willingness to speak in my presence.

Bear

108   *Bear*   Gratitude to the black bear rolling in a stream near the western edge of Waterton Lake in traditional and sacred Siksikaitsitapi (Blackfoot) territory. Our encounter with him was full of wildness, even as it was also too close for comfort and safety.

Lake Champlain at Flood Level

110   *Lake Champlain at Flood Level*   I wrote this poem after the century flood (the highest water in a hundred years) of April and May 2011 on Lake Champlain, unceded ancestral Abenaki territory. Now, as I write this note, Vermont is still repairing damage from the floods of July 2023 and '24. The small organic farmers who work the rich soils in the delta just east of where the Winooski River meets Lake Champlain found their fields four feet underwater in early July of both '23 and '24. They say that they never imagined farming

through a flood bigger than the one of 2011. And then the
water rose and rose and rose.

A Murmuration of Dreams

112   *our bodies*   Gratitude to Alexis Pauline Gumbs for her
book *Undrowned: Black Feminist Lessons from Marine
Mammals*. Gumbs's words make possible the last dozen lines
of this poem.

Inside Grief Time

113   *Coya   Diane   Amber   Laura   Becca   Karl*   This poem
originates from multiple powerful rituals of calling of the
names, one of which I describe earlier in "A Cluster of Practices: An Introduction" (xvi). I'm also indebted here to
Melvin Dixon's keynote in 1992 at Outwrite, a queer writers' conference. Dixon—Black, gay, disabled, and sick with
AIDS—knew he wasn't going to live much longer. The re-
frain of his keynote was "I'll be somewhere listening for my
name." I can still hear him singing the Black spiritual this
line comes from, still feel the ache in my chest. For the text
of his speech, see Dixon, "I'll Be Somewhere Listening for
My Name." For a powerful unfolding of the Black queer
traditions Dixon was speaking from, see Gumbs, "Helping
Each Other Feel Possible."

Turning Toward Each Other

117   *into existence*   As I think about naming and writing ourselves into existence, I turn again to Audre Lorde. She tells
us: "Poetry is the way we help give name to the nameless so
it can be thought" (Lorde, *Sister Outsider*, 37).

117   *with queer and trans disabled people*   Gratitudes to the people and books who helped me begin to turn toward queer/
trans disability communities: Robin Earth sat on the front
stoop with me; Ethan Thomas Young opened the door for
me; *No More Stares* handed me a mirror (Freeman et al.,
No More Stares); *With the Power of Each Breath: A Disabled Women's Anthology* gave me the word and concept of
ableism (Browne et al., *With the Power of Each Breath*); Alexander Bear Goodrum and Diana Courvant bridged trans
community and disability community with me in the late
1990s and early 2000s when that work had barely begun.

117   *pry bars*   As I think of transforming ourselves, each other, and the world—using poems as pry bars—I turn to Laura Hershey. She tells us: "Poetry aims for the thing itself, not just to name the thing. Poetry draws a straight line connecting the desire, the request, the fulfillment. Poetry *is* power of words to effect change, to move people" (Hershey, "Getting Comfortable," 132).

119   *conjure them*   As I think of the work of turning toward each other, of gathering, I turn to Leah Lakshmi Piepzna-Samarasinha. They tell us: "Prefigurative politics is a fancy term for the idea of imagining and building the world we want to see now. It's waking up and acting as if the revolution has happened. . . . As a performer and curator/producer, I believe that how you do it and who is there to see it is as important as what is on the stage. My favorite performance spaces are spaces that become temporary, two-hour communities that are autonomous zones that feel like freedom" (Piepzna-Samarasinha, *Care Work*, 149–50).

Bibliography

Acton, Kelsie. "Plain Language for Disability Culture." In *Crip Authorship: Disability as Method*, edited by Maura Mills and Rebecca Sanchez, 58–72. New York: New York University Press, 2023.

Adams, David Wallace. *Education for Extinction: American Indians and the Boarding School Experience, 1875–1928*. 2nd ed. Lawrence: University Press of Kansas, 2020.

Autistic Self Advocacy Network. "One Idea per Line: A Guide to Making Easy Read Resources." Accessed May 29, 2024. https://autisticadvocacy.org/wp-content/uploads/2021/07/One-Idea-Per-Line.pdf.

Baggs, Mel. "About." *Amelia Evelyn Voicy Baggs: Poetry and Creative Writing* (blog). Accessed November 1, 2023. https://ameliabaggs.wordpress.com/about/.

Baggs, Mel. "Empty Mirrors and Redwoods." *Ballastexistenz* (blog), May 12, 2014. https://ballastexistenz.wordpress.com/2014/05/12/empty-mirrors-and-redwoods/.

Baggs, Mel. "In My Language." YouTube video, posted January 14, 2007. 8 min., 34 sec. https://www.youtube.com/watch?v=JnylM1hI2jc.

Baggs, Mel. "Up in the Clouds and Down in the Valley: My Richness and Yours." *Disability Studies Quarterly* 30, no. 1 (2010). https://doi.org/10.18061/dsq.v30i1.1052.

Ben-Moshe, Liat. *Decarcerating Disability: Deinstitionalization and Prison Abolition*. Minneapolis: University of Minnesota Press, 2020.

Ben-Moshe, Liat, Chris Chapman, and Allison C. Carey, eds. *Disability Incarcerated: Imprisonment and Disability*. New York: Palgrave Macmillan, 2015.

Benoit, Virgil, and David Marshall, eds. *Treaty at Old Crossing: To Invite Enlightened Understanding; Reflections, Writings and Responses to the 1863 Treaty, Notes and Dialogue*. Red Lake Falls, MN: Association of the French of the North, 2008.

Brashear, Regan, dir. *Fixed: The Science/Fiction of Human Enhancement*. Oakland, CA: Making Change Media, 2013. DVD.

brown, adrienne maree. "Outro." In *Octavia's Brood: Science Fiction Stories from Social Justice Movements*, edited by Walidah Imarisha and adrienne maree brown, 279–81. Oakland, CA: AK, 2015.

Browne, Susan, Debra Connors, and Nanci Stern, eds. *With the Power of Each Breath: A Disabled Women's Anthology*. Pittsburgh: Cleis, 1985.

Burch, Susan. *Committed: Remembering Native Kinship in and Beyond Institutions*. Chapel Hill: University of North Carolina Press, 2021.

Carr, Cynthia. *Fire in the Belly: The Life and Times of David Wojnarowicz*. New York: Bloomsbury USA, 2013.

Carter, Angela M. "Teaching with Trauma: Disability Pedagogy, Feminism, and the Trigger Warnings Debate." *Disability Studies Quarterly* 35, no. 2 (2015). https://doi .org/10.18061/dsq.v35i2.4652.

Chen, Mel Y. "Chronic Illness, Slowness, and the Time of Writing." In *Crip Authorship: Disability as Method*, edited by Maura Mills and Rebecca Sanchez, 33–37. New York: New York University Press, 2023.

Chen, Mel Y., Alison Kafer, Eunjung Kim, and Julie Avril Minich, eds. *Crip Genealogies*. Durham, NC: Duke University Press, 2023.

Child, Brenda J. *Boarding School Seasons: American Indian Families, 1900–1940*. Lincoln: University of Nebraska Press, 1998.

Clare, Eli. *Brilliant Imperfection: Grappling with Cure*. Durham, NC: Duke University Press, 2017.

Clare, Eli. *Exile and Pride: Disability, Queerness, and Liberation*. 2nd ed. Cambridge, MA: South End, 2009.

Clarren, Rebecca. *The Cost of Free Land: Jews, Lakota, and an American Inheritance*. New York: Viking, 2023.

Curtis, Ted, Robert Dellar, Esther Leslie, and Ben Watson, eds. *Mad Pride*. Self-published, Chipmunka, 2011.

Deer, Sarah. *The Beginning and End of Rape: Confronting Sexual Violence in Native America*. Minneapolis: University of Minnesota Press, 2015.

Dixon, Ejeris, and Leah Lakshmi Piepzna-Samarasinha, eds. *Beyond Survival: Strategies and Stories from the Transformative Justice Movement*. Chico, CA: AK, 2020.

Dixon, Melvin. "I'll Be Somewhere Listening for My Name." In *Outwrite: The Speeches That Shaped LGBTQ Literary Culture*, edited by Julie R. Enszer and Elena Gross, 101–7. New Brunswick, NJ: Rutgers University Press, 2022.

Dolmage, Jay. *Academic Ableism: Disability and Higher Education*. Ann Arbor: University of Michigan Press, 2017.

Dunbar-Ortiz, Roxanne. *An Indigenous Peoples' History of the United States*. Boston: Beacon, 2014.

Dunbar-Ortiz, Roxanne. *Not "A Nation of Immigrants": Settler Colonialism, White Supremacy, and a History of Erasure and Exclusion*. Boston: Beacon, 2021.

Ellis, JJJJJerome. *The Clearing*. Brooklyn: Wendy's Subway, 2021.

Erickson, Loree. "Thinking About and with Collective Care." *Cultivating Collective Care* (blog), June 17, 2020. https://www.cultivatingcollectivecare.com/post/thinking -about-and-with-collective-care.

Ferguson, Philip M., Dianne L. Ferguson, and Meredith M. Brodsky. *"Away from the Public Gaze": A History of the Fairview Training Center and the Institutionalization of People with Developmental Disabilities in Oregon*. Monmouth, OR: Teaching Research Institute, 2008. https://mn.gov/mnddc/parallels2/pdf/00s/08/08-Fairview_Report.pdf.

France, David, dir. *How to Survive a Plague*. New York: Public Square Films, 2012. DVD.

Freeman, Ann Cupolo, Corbett Joan O'Toole, and Victoria Lewis. *No More Stares*. Berkeley, CA: Disability Rights Education and Defense Fund, 1982.

Goldberg, Carey. "For These Trailblazers, Wheelchairs Matter." *New York Times*, August 17, 2000. https://www.nytimes.com/2000/08/17/us/for-these-trailblazers-wheelchairs -matter.html.

Gonzalez, Mario, and Elizabeth Cook-Lynn. *The Politics of Hallowed Ground: Wounded Knee and the Struggle for Indian Sovereignty*. Champaign: University of Illinois Press, 1999.

Gorman, Rachel. "Mad Nation? Thinking Through Race, Class, and Mad Identity Politics." In *Mad Matters: A Critical Reader in Canadian Mad Studies*, edited by Brenda A. LeFrançois, Robert Menzies, and Geoffrey Reaume, 269–80. Toronto, ON: Canadian Scholars, 2013.

Graybill, Andrew R. "Rangers, Mounties, and the Subjugation of Indigenous Peoples, 1870–1885." *Great Plains Quarterly* 24, no. 2 (2004): 83–100.

Gregory, Anne. "Competency, Allotment, and the Canton Asylum: The Case of a Muscogee Woman." *Disability Studies Quarterly* 41, no. 4 (2021). https://doi.org/10.18061 /dsq.v41i4.8476.

Gumbs, Alexis Pauline. "Helping Each Other Feel Possible: Dr. Alexis Pauline Gumbs on Audre Lorde and Melvin Dixon." *The Reckoning*, April 4, 2023. https://www.the reckoningmag.com/podcast/helping-each-other-feel-possible-dr-alexis-pauline-gumbs -on-audre-lorde-and-melvin-dixon-5fa6a?rq=gumbs#gs.okwbsk=.

Gumbs, Alexis Pauline. *Undrowned: Black Feminist Lessons from Marine Mammals*. Chico, CA: AK, 2020.

Hamraie, Aimi. *Building Access: Universal Design and the Politics of Disability*. Minneapolis: University of Minnesota Press, 2017.

Hernández, Kelly Lytle. *City of Inmates: Conquest, Rebellion, and the Rise of Human Caging in Los Angeles, 1771–1965*. Chapel Hill: University of North Carolina Press, 2017.

Hersey, Tricia. *Rest Is Resistance: A Manifesto*. New York: Little, Brown Spark, 2022.

Hershey, Laura. "Getting Comfortable." In *Beauty Is a Verb: The New Poetry of Disability*, edited by Jennifer Bartlett, Sheila Black, and Michael Northen, 129–32. El Paso, TX: Cinco Puntos, 2011.

Hixson, Walter L. *American Settler Colonialism: A History*. New York: Palgrave Macmillan, 2013.

Hollibaugh, Amber. *My Dangerous Desires: A Queer Girl Dreaming Her Way Home*. Durham, NC: Duke University Press, 2000.

Hurwitz, Laura, and Shawn Bourque. "Settler Colonial Primer." *Unsettling America: Decolonization in Theory and Practice* (blog), June 6, 2014. https://unsettlingamerica .wordpress.com/2014/06/06/settler-colonialism-primer/.

Imarisha, Walidah. "Introduction." In *Octavia's Brood: Science Fiction Stories from Social Justice Movements*, edited by Walidah Imarisha and adrienne maree brown, 3–5. Oakland, CA: AK, 2015.

James, Tyler. "The Fairview Training Center May Have the Darkest History in Oregon." *That Oregon Life*, July 3, 2015; updated October 2019. https://thatoregonlife.com /2015/07/the-fairview-training-center-may-have-the-darkest-history-in-oregon/.

Jawort, Adrian. "Genocide by Other Means: U.S. Army Slaughtered Buffalo in Plains Indian Wars." *Indian Country Today*, May 9, 2011. http://indiancountrytodaymedia network.com/2011/05/09/genocide-other-means-us-army-slaughtered-buffalo-plains -indian-wars-30798.

Jones, Jacqueline. "Labor and the Idea of Race in the American South." *Journal of Southern History* 75, no. 3 (2009): 613–26.

Kadi, Joe. *The Great Loss of the Twentieth Century*. Self-published, Lulu.com, 2023.

Kadi, Joe. "Stupidity 'Deconstructed.'" In *Thinking Class: Sketches from a Cultural Worker*, 39–57. Boston: South End, 1996.

Kafai, Shayda. *Crip Kinship: The Disability Justice and Art Activism of Sins Invalid*. Vancouver: Arsenal Pulp, 2021.

Kafer, Alison. "After Crip, Crip After." *South Atlantic Quarterly* 120, no. 2 (2021): 415–34.

Kafer, Alison. *Feminist, Queer, Crip*. Bloomington: Indiana University Press, 2013.

Kafer, Alison. "Fixed: The Science/Fiction of Human Enhancement." *Disability Studies Quarterly* 35, no. 4 (2015). https://doi.org/10.18061/.v35i4.4985.

Kafer, Alison. "Un/Safe Disclosures: Scenes of Disability and Trauma." *Journal of Literary and Cultural Disability Studies* 10, no. 1 (2016): 1–20.

Kauanui, J. Kēhaulani. "'A Structure, Not an Event': Settler Colonialism and Enduring Indigeneity." *Lateral* 5, no. 1 (2016). https://csalateral.org/issue/5-1/forum-alt -humanities-settler-colonialism-enduring-indigeneity-kauanui/.

Kelley, Robin D. G. *Freedom Dreams: The Black Radical Imagination*. Boston: Beacon, 2022.

Kim, Eunjung. *Curative Violence: Rehabilitating Disability, Gender, and Sexuality in Modern Korea*. Durham, NC: Duke University Press, 2016.

Kim, Eunjung. "Unbecoming Human: An Ethics of Objects." *GLQ: A Journal of Lesbian and Gay Studies* 21, no. 2 (2015): 295–320.

Kim, Jina. "'People of the Apokalis': Spatial Disability and the Bhopal Disaster." *Disability Studies Quarterly* 34, no. 3 (2014). https://doi.org/10.18061/dsq.v34i3.3795.

Kim, Jina, and Sami Schalk. "Reclaiming the Radical Politics of Self-Care: A Crip-of-Color Critique." *South Atlantic Quarterly* 120, no. 2 (2021): 325–42.

Kimmerer, Robin Wall. *Braiding Sweetgrass: Indigenous Wisdom, Scientific Knowledge, and the Teachings of Plants*. Minneapolis: Milkweed, 2013.

Koford, Amelia. "Engaging an Author in a Critical Reading of Subject Headings." *Journal of Critical Library and Information Studies* 1, no. 1 (2017). https://doi.org/10.24242 /jclis.v1i1.20.

Kunzel, Regina. "Queer History, Mad History, and the Politics of Health." *American Quarterly* 69, no. 2 (2017): 315–19.

landry, danielle, Jenna Reid, Jijian Voronka, becky mcfarlane, kathryn Church, david Reville, and anonymous, eds. "Toronto: How Do We Win?" *Asylum: The Magazine of Democratic Psychiatry* 20, no. 4 (2013). https://asylummagazine.org/wp-content /uploads/2019/09/Asylum-20.4-2013-Mad-in-Toronto_compressed.pdf.

LeFrançois, Brenda A., Robert Menzies, and Geoffrey Reaume, eds. *Mad Matters: A Critical Reader in Canadian Mad Studies*. Toronto: Canadian Scholars', 2013.

Levins Morales, Aurora. "Cripping the Great Turning: Imagining Disability Justice." Public Talk, Smith College, October 13, 2022.

Levins Morales, Aurora. *The Story of What Is Broken Is Whole: An Aurora Levins Morales Reader*. Durham, NC: Duke University Press, 2024.

Levins Morales, Aurora. "Torturers." In *Medicine Stories*, 111–14. Cambridge, MA: South End, 1998.

Lewis, Talila A. "the birth of resistance: courageous dreams, powerful nobodies & revolutionary madness." In *Resistance and Hope: Essays by Disabled People; Crip*

Wisdom for the People, edited by Alice Wong. San Francisco: Disability Visibility Project, 2018.

Lewis, Talila A. "Working Definition of Ableism—January 2022 Update." *Turning into Self* (blog), January 1, 2022. https://www.talilalewis.com/blog/working-definition-of -ableism-january-2022-update.

Lomawaima, K. Tsianina, Bryan McKinley Jones Brayboy, and Teresa L. McCarty. "Editors' Introduction to the Special Issue: Native American Boarding School Stories." *Journal of American Indian Education* 57, no. 1 (2018): 1–10.

Lorde, Audre. *Sister Outsider: Essays and Speeches*. Berkeley, CA: Crossing, 1984.

Luterman, Sara. "Plain Language Translation of *Disability Visibility: First-Person Stories from the Twenty-First Century*." Disability Visibility Project, June 30, 2020. https://docs.google.com/document/d/180BSG2IEZHNOPhp9uH7dG_N6YLe9e NvkeS_ry6tEZJo/edit.

Mays, Kyle T. *An Afro-Indigenous History of the United States*. Boston: Beacon, 2021.

Meronek, Toshio, and Miss Major Griffin-Gracy. *Miss Major Speaks: Conversations with a Black Trans Revolutionary*. Brooklyn: Verso, 2023.

Mingus, Mia. "Access Intimacy: The Missing Link." *Leaving Evidence* (blog), May 5, 2011. https://leavingevidence.wordpress.com/2011/05/05/access-intimacy-the-missing-link/.

National Archives. "Homestead Act (1862)." Accessed July 29, 2021. https://www .archives.gov/milestone-documents/homestead-act.

Nishida, Akemi. *Just Care: Messy Entanglements of Disability, Dependency, and Desire*. Philadelphia: Temple University Press, 2022.

Northeast Passage. "Trek to Galehead." Accessed November 18, 2023. https://www .nepassage.org/trek-galehead.

Oregon Council on Developmental Disabilities. "Voices from Fairview." YouTube video, posted November 19, 2014. 17 min., 30 sec. https://www.youtube.com/watch ?v=GP85pIcBQQ8.

Ortiz, Naomi. *Rituals for Climate Change: A Crip Struggle for Ecojustice*. Goleta, CA: Punctum, 2023.

Ortiz, Naomi. *Sustaining Spirit: Self-Care for Social Justice*. Berkeley, CA: Reclamation, 2018.

Ostler, Jeffrey. *The Plains Sioux and U.S. Colonialism from Lewis and Clark to Wounded Knee*. Cambridge: Cambridge University Press, 2004.

O'Toole, Corbett Joan. *Fading Scars: My Queer Disability History*. Fort Worth, TX: Autonomous, 2015.

Pelka, Fred. *What We Have Done: An Oral History of the Disability Rights Movement*. Amherst: University of Massachusetts Press, 2011.

Pharr, Suzanne. *Transformation: Toward a People's Democracy.* Edited by Christian Matheis. Blacksburg: Virginia Tech Publishing, 2021. https://www.suzannepharr.com/transformation-book-options/.

Piepzna-Samarasinha, Leah Lakshmi. *Bodymap.* Toronto: Mawenzi House, 2015.

Piepzna-Samarasinha, Leah Lakshmi. *Care Work: Dreaming Disability Justice.* Vancouver: Arsenal Pulp, 2018.

Piepzna-Samarasinha, Leah Lakshmi. *The Future Is Disabled: Prophecies, Love Notes, and Mourning Songs.* Vancouver: Arsenal Pulp, 2022.

Piepzna-Samarasinha, Leah Lakshmi, and Alice Wong. "#StaceyTaughtUs Syllabus: Work by Stacey Park Milbern." Disability Visibility Project, May 23, 2020. https://disabilityvisibilityproject.com/2020/05/23/staceytaughtus-syllabus-work-by-stacey-milbern-park/.

Price, Margaret. "The Bodymind Problem and the Possibilities of Pain." *Hypatia* 30, no. 1 (2015): 268–84.

Price, Margaret. *Crip Spacetime: Access, Failure, and Accountability in Academic Life.* Durham, NC: Duke University Press, 2024.

Raffo, Susan. *Liberated to the Bone: Histories, Bodies, Futures.* Chico, CA: AK, 2022.

Ray, Sarah Jaquette, and Jay Sibara, eds. *Disability Studies and the Environmental Humanities: Toward an Eco-Crip Theory.* Lincoln: University of Nebraska Press, 2017.

Red Lake Nation. "Tribal History & Historical Photos." Accessed November 11, 2023. https://www.redlakenation.org/tribal-history-historical-photos/.

Rowe, Daniel J. "Humble Intellectual Leaves Unique Legacy." *Eastern Door*, February 7, 2019. https://easterndoor.com/2019/02/07/humble-intellectual-leaves-unique-legacy/.

Ryan, Mackenzie. "The Best Signs from Iowa's National School Walkout Rally." *Des Moines Register*, April 20, 2018. https://www.desmoinesregister.com/story/news/education/2018/04/20/11-signs-iowa-students-protest-gun-violence-call-gun-control-measures/537007002/.

Samuels, Ellen. "Six Ways of Looking at Crip Time." *Disability Studies Quarterly* 37, no. 3 (2017). https://doi.org/10.18061/dsq.v37i3.5824.

Samuels, Ellen, and Elizabeth Freeman. "Introduction: Crip Temporalities." *South Atlantic Quarterly* 120, no. 2 (2021): 245–54.

San Francisco State University. "Patient No More." Accessed November 11, 2023. https://longmoreinstitute.sfsu.edu/patient-no-more.

San Francisco State University. "Section 504 Protest Mural." Accessed November 17, 2023. https://longmoreinstitute.sfsu.edu/patient-no-more/section-504-protest-mural.

Schalk, Sami. *Bodyminds Reimagined: (Dis)ability, Race, and Gender in Black Women's Speculative Fiction.* Durham, NC: Duke University Press, 2018.

Schalk, Sami. "More Than Just Prevention: The NBWHP and the Black Disability Politics of HIV/AIDS." In *Black Disability Politics*, 110–28. Durham, NC: Duke University Press, 2022.

Schneider, Beth E., and Nancy Stoller. *Women Resisting AIDS: Feminist Strategies of Empowerment*. Philadelphia: Temple University Press, 1995.

Schulman, Sarah. *Let the Record Show: A Political History of ACT UP New York, 1987–1993*. New York: Farrar, Straus and Giroux, 2021.

Sequenzia, Amy, and Elizabeth J. Grace, eds. *Typed Words, Loud Hands*. Fort Worth, TX: Autonomous, 2015.

Shilts, Randy. *The Mayor of Castro Street: The Life and Times of Harvey Milk*. New York: St. Martin's, 1980.

Sins Invalid. "Language Justice Is Disability Justice." Accessed May 31, 2024. https://www.sinsinvalid.org/news-1/2021/6/8/la-justicia-de-lenguaje-es-justicia-para-personas-con-discapacidadeslanguage-justice-is-disability-justice.

Stange, Margit. "'Patient No More' Show in Berkeley Documents a Historic Disability Rights Protest." *Berkeleyside*, November 9, 2015. https://www.berkeleyside.org/2015/11/09/patient-no-more-show-in-berkeley-documents-an-historic-disability-rights-protest.

Strub, Sean. *Body Counts: A Memoir of Activism, Sex, and Survival*. New York: Simon and Schuster, 2014.

Sullivan, Carolyn. "Contextualizing Disability: A Century of Library of Congress Subject Headings." *Emerging Library and Information Perspectives* 4, no. 1 (2021): 8–33.

Sweet Honey in the Rock. "Legendary Civil Rights Singers, Sweet Honey in the Rock: Part 1 of a *Democracy Now!* Special." Interview with Amy Goodman. *Democracy Now!*, May 29, 2003. https://www.democracynow.org/2003/5/29/legendary_civil_rights_singers_sweet_honey.

Taylor, Sunaura. *Disabled Ecologies: Lessons from a Wounded Desert*. Oakland: University of California Press, 2024.

Trafzer, Clifford E., Jean A. Keller, and Lorene Sisquoc. *Boarding School Blues: Revisiting American Indian Educational Experiences*. Lincoln: University of Nebraska Press, 2006.

Treuer, David. *The Heartbeat of Wounded Knee: Native America from 1890 to the Present*. New York: Riverhead Books, 2019.

University of British Columbia. "About X̱wi7x̱wa Library." Accessed October 25, 2024. https://xwi7xwa.library.ubc.ca/about/.

Veracini, Lorenzo. "Settler Colonialism Is Not Finished." In *The Settler Colonial Present*, edited by Lorenzo Veracini, 68–94. London: Palgrave Macmillan, 2015.

Vizenor, Gerald Robert. *Manifest Manners: Narratives on Postindian Survivance*. Lincoln: University of Nebraska Press, 2010.

Vizenor, Gerald Robert. *Survivance: Narratives of Native Presence*. Lincoln: University of Nebraska Press, 2009.

Voyles, Traci Brynne. *Wastelanding: Legacies of Uranium Mining in Navajo Country*. Minneapolis: University of Minnesota Press, 2015.

Wald, Gayle F. *Shout, Sister, Shout! The Untold Story of Rock-and-Roll Trailblazer Sister Rosetta Tharpe*. Boston: Beacon, 2007.

Watkis-Hayes, Celeste. *Remaking a Life: How Women Living with HIV/AIDS Confront Inequality*. Oakland: University of California Press, 2019.

Weihs, Jean. "A Tribute to Brian Deer." *Technicalities* 39, no. 3 (2019): 11–12.

White, Richard. *"It's Your Misfortune and None of My Own": A New History of the American West*. Norman: University of Oklahoma Press, 1991.

Whitt, Sarah. "'Care and Maintenance': Indigeneity, Disability and Settler Colonialism at the Canton Asylum for Insane Indians, 1902–1934." *Disability Studies Quarterly* 41, no. 4 (2021). https://doi.org/10.18061/dsq.v41i4.8463.

Wilm, Julius. "'The Indians Must Yield': Antebellum Free Land, the Homestead Act, and the Displacement of Native Peoples." *Great Plains Quarterly* 38, no. 1 (2018): 1–23.

Wolfe, Patrick. "Settler Colonialism and the Elimination of the Native." *Journal of Genocide Research* 8, no. 4 (2006): 387–409.

Wong, Alice, ed. *Disability Visibility: First-Person Stories from the Twenty-First Century*. New York: Vintage, 2020.

Woolford, Andrew John. *This Benevolent Experiment: Indigenous Boarding Schools, Genocide, and Redress in Canada and the United States*. Lincoln: University of Nebraska Press, 2015.

Yellow Bird, Pemina. "Wild Indians: Native Perspectives on the Hiawatha Asylum for Insane Indians." National Empowerment Center. Accessed October 24, 2024. https://power2u.org/wp-content/uploads/2017/01/NativePerspectivesPeminaYellowBird.pdf.

York, Jake Adam. "A Murmuration of Starlings." In *A Murmuration of Starlings*, 52–61. Carbondale: Southern Illinois University Press, 2008.

Index